PROTESTANT FAITH AND RELIGIOUS LIBERTY

PROTESTANT
FAITH
AND
RELIGIOUS
LIBERTY

PHILIP WOGAMAN

NASHVILLE **ABINGDON PRESS** NEW YORK

TO CAROLYN

PREFACE

The problem of this book may be stated as follows: Why should Christians support a public policy of religious freedom? And, on the basis of the answer, what should the applications and limitations of that policy be? Necessarily, therefore, the book is concerned with the Christian's whole orientation, as a Christian, to the state and things political.

In the light of this statement of the problem and in the spirit of the new ecumenical era, the title of this volume may seem arrogant. Does one really suppose that *"Protestant* faith" is simply interchangeable with *"Christian* faith," as though only Protestants were to be thought of as Christian? Is this to be a reversion to pre-ecumenical thinking on church-state relations, with thinly veiled overtones of hostility toward Roman Catholicism as the supposed chief sinner against religious liberty?

Such is far from my intention. The title must rather be related to two purposes of writing. First, it is designed as a contribution to the clarification of Protestant thought on

7

religious liberty. Protestants must seek such clarification in order to be more fully equipped to participate in the emerging dialogue with Roman Catholicism, Eastern Orthodoxy, and the non-Christian faiths. Protestantism is, indeed, grappling with the issues of religious liberty in fresh ways. But its lack of consensus on church-state relations is becoming increasingly apparent and can no longer be evaded if Protestantism is to participate responsibly and creatively in ecumenical conversations.

The second purpose is to suggest that Protestant faith is a permanent *aspect* of the Christian faith. Even if Protestantism as a distinct, historical religious movement should lose its existence in a universal Christian fellowship, this aspect will be important. The very possibility of there being such a fellowship requires the inclusion of those aspects of Christian witness of which Protestantism has been the chief steward. This permanent Protestant element, then, actually has a claim upon all Christians. Within ecumenical Protestantism the phrase "truly catholic, truly evangelical, truly reformed" is emerging to describe the church as it ought to be in its wholeness. To be truly reformed is to be permanently Protestant, although the Protestant aspect of the church is but one aspect of its fuller meaning. It may be argued, however, that those aspects of historic Protestantism which account for its existence in separation from Roman Catholicism are also the most decisive Christian grounds for a doctrine of religious liberty—even though there are other elements in Christian faith which are also relevant. This is to suggest that the doctrine of religious liberty may be a more distinctively Protestant contribution to the ecumenical dialogue —just as Roman Catholicism and Eastern Orthodoxy have their treasures to offer an incomplete Protestantism in the emerging whole church.

It is by no means a simple matter to relate basic theological doctrines to questions of social policy. Christian social ethics, whose business it is to venture such correlations, must be especially aware of the diversity of uses to which a given doctrine may be put. Christians of presumed equal integrity have been on opposite sides of most political controversy. The Christianity which produced Richard the Lion-Hearted and Torquemada sent St. Francis to speak with love to the Saracen. The faith of the apostle Paul was ultimately an important factor in ending slavery and, through Calvinism, had great effect on the development of democracy. Yet Paul himself applied the faith conservatively in urging slaves to obey their masters and in regarding the duly (but not responsibly) constituted authorities as having been instituted by God. This should remind us that a great religious leader may not himself grasp the full practical logic of his own central doctrines.

For this reason it may be less justifiable to quote Luther and Calvin on the church-state issues they faced in their time than it is to seek the most logical application of their *central* affirmations. Few men are perfectly consistent. In some respects even the most daring innovator remains a child of his time. Moreover, great ideas or religious faiths can hardly be born into conditions immediately receptive to their fullest practical consequences. Whether or not Paul clearly understood the incompatibility of slavery with the Christian faith (which is doubtful), it would have been idle for him to attempt its destruction.

In searching for the elements of Protestant faith which are decisive in relation to religious liberty, the best approach is therefore less one of adding and comparing what great Protestant theologians have said on the subject than one of seeking fresh application of their most central insights as Protestant theologians. Recent research (I shall refer especially to the work of Thomas G. Sanders) demonstrates the wide diversity of Protestant church-state conceptions, and it may even suggest the irreconcilability of some historic Protestant positions on religious liberty. But a more important question for Protestants is whether or not there is an essential core of meaning, a "Protestant principle," to use Tillich's phrase, which has decisive implications when applied to the problem of religious liberty. I believe there is, although it must be acknowledged here that any attempt to say what Protestant faith *essentially* is must necessarily be interpretative. I hope that the interpretation of Protestant faith which appears on these pages will be shared by different kinds of Protestants as they reflect upon their various traditions.

It is the thesis of this volume that the Reformation doctrine of the sovereignty of God provides the most important clue to the inner meaning of Protestantism on the one hand, and to the basis of religious liberty in Christian theology on the other. Negatively, the sovereignty of God stands in judgment upon every absolute identification of God with what is less than God (idolatry) and upon every human pretension of infallibility. If God is sovereign and transcendent of his creation (as the reformers emphatically held) then no man can claim perfect understanding of God (as the reformers sometimes forgot!). Positively, if God is sovereign he may disclose himself to any man at any time or place in ways which it would be blasphemous for any other man or political institution to prejudge. As I shall suggest in due course, the issue of religious liberty may be understood theologically in terms of the freedom of God quite as well as the freedom of man in matters of religion—God's freedom to speak through every man, in accents both familiar and strange and with meanings which are both positive and negative. The classical Reformation emphases upon justification by faith and the priesthood of all believers may be understood as required by this conception of God and his ways with man.

The issues which must be considered in relation to this theme are complex. They cannot be dealt with properly by Christian theology as an isolated field of study. Like all other work in Christian social ethics, the present essay is written at the intersection of several fields of study. It is, accordingly, dependent upon the work of different kinds of specialists. As one whose work is typically at the juncture of widely disparate fields, I am only too aware of my dependence in each of these fields upon more authoritative writers. To combine the insights of, for example, theology, political science, sociology, and political philosophy may seem a pretentious business. Yet it is a necessary one if Christian faith is to find relevant application in the real world. I venture this task, with the conviction that shortcomings will be corrected by others, to the greater glory of God and with a deep sense of gratitude to all those who have in various ways contributed to the writing and the thought which has preceded it.

PHILIP WOGAMAN

Wesley Theological Seminary
Washington, D. C,

ACKNOWLEDGMENTS

I wish to thank the following publishers who have generously granted permission to quote material from their publications:

Association Press, New York, for quotations from *The Basis of Religious Liberty*, by A F. Carrillo de Albornoz.

Harper & Row, Publishers, Inc., New York and Evanston, for quotations from *Radical Monotheism and Western Culture*, by H. Richard Niebuhr.

Holt, Rinehart and Winston, Inc., New York, for quotations from *Protestant Concepts of Church and State*, by Thomas G. Sanders.

Sheed and Ward, Inc., New York, for quotations from *We Hold These Truths: Catholic Reflections on the American Proposition*, by John Courtney Murray, S. J.

University of California Press, Berkeley, for quotations from *The Paradoxes of Freedom*, by Sidney Hook.

The University of Chicago Press, for quotations from *The Protestant Era*, by Paul Tillich, and from the article, "The Constitutionality of Public Aid to Parochial

13

Schools," by Robert F. Drinan, in *The Wall Between Church and State*, edited by Dallin H. Oaks.

Grateful acknowledgment is also made to several journals for the use here of some of the material which I have previously written in articles in these publications:

The Christian Century, for "The Amish Affair and Religious Liberty," April 13, 1966;

A Journal of Church and State, for "The Changing Role of Government and the Myth of Separation," V (May, 1963), 61-76;

Religion and the Public Order, 1964 (Chicago: The University of Chicago Press, 1965), for "The NCC National Study Conference on Church and State," pp. 121-48.

I am grateful to Walter G. Muelder for permission to quote from his unpublished 1962 Colliver Lectures on "Church and State in the Responsible Society" at the University of the Pacific.

I wish to thank Grover C. Bagby, Paul K. Deats, Jr., Dean M. Kelley, and Tex S. Semple, who read all or parts of this book in manuscript form. I benefited greatly from their suggestions even though they are not, of course, to be held responsible for the contents.

I wish finally to record my gratitude to my wife, to whom this book is dedicated, for her unfailing support and encouragement in this and all my endeavors.

CONTENTS

15

CONTENTS

I

A Perennial Question in a New Era

The history of religious coercion, persecution, and intolerance is a very old one. It may be as old as man himself. It is at least as old as religious diversity and conflict.

1. A Very Old and Very Contemporary Problem

Three millennia of Western history present a vast panorama of such religious conflict and persecution. The highlights are well known to all of us: the struggle over monotheism in ancient Egypt; the bloody suppression of the idolator in Israel; the trial and execution of Socrates; the suffering and martyrdom of heretics under Christians; the rise of a militantly intolerant Islam; the crusades of Christians against Moslems; periodic pogroms against Jews; the Inquisition; the vicious bloodletting of the religious wars between Protestants and Catholics; the persecution of "witches"; and so on.

No one can calculate the evil and waste which has resulted from such repression. Nor can anyone point to a time when it began and say that this is where and how mankind lost religious liberty, for it is doubtful that religious liberty ever had a golden age. Even the idea of religious liberty seems to be of comparatively recent origin. As Professor Ruffini once remarked, the idea of religious liberty is curiously absent from the literature of the Greeks and Romans, even in relation to their concepts of liberty in general.[1] The same judgment applies to other ancient peoples, such as the Hebrews. Whenever the ancients sought religious liberty, it was generally religious liberty for themselves. And once they had enough power to secure it for themselves they were seldom reluctant to persecute others.

Nor is religious coercion simply a historical issue. Openly or subtly, it is very real in the contemporary world—even though it is now clearly on the defensive, and even though some who persecute others for religious reasons may not be aware of what they are doing. Patterns of relationship are everywhere in flux, but some generalizations can safely be made concerning religious persecution and religious liberty in various parts of the world at the present time:[2]

In predominantly Roman Catholic countries, the situation has improved considerably in the past generation. The process of liberalization has noticeably quickened since the reign of Pope John XXIII and the beginning of *aggiornamento* and the Second Vatican Council. In such countries as Colombia, which used to provide some of the worst examples of religious repression in the world, new ecumenical winds of reconciliation have recently been symbolized by joint Catholic-Protestant services of prayer and singing. Nevertheless, in almost all Roman Catholic countries non-Catholic persons suffer some legal and political disabilities ranging from a religious test for public office to problems concerning marriage and public "proselytizing." Practical administration of law varies widely, of course. Religious coercion remains a very serious problem in Spain and Haiti. In the former land, *private* worship by non-Catholics is alone acceptable, and there has been considerable resistance to liberalization (although there has also been considerable support for change, even within the hierarchy). In Haiti a corrupt dictatorship almost without parallel on earth suppresses the religious liberty of Protestant and Catholic alike on the grounds that their churches are involved in anti-government plotting. The possibilities for change in that unhappy land seem as remote as the need for change is urgent, and in seeking change Catholics and Protestants may well find a common cause.

The adoption by the Vatican Council of a Declaration on Religious Liberty has been hailed widely as a major step forward in Roman Catholicism. The Declaration, as I shall suggest later, needs to be viewed in the context of an ongoing dialogue. Its adequacy as a final Christian statement of the problem of religious liberty must be subjected to the closest scrutiny in that dialogue. Nevertheless, its practical effects will undoubtedly be profound. The judgment that the Vatican Council has, as one prelate put it, done "irreparable good," unquestionably applies also to the major product of the Council in the area of religious liberty. It is a manifest of the good intentions in this area of the large majority of bishops of the church. But even if this were not so, it has supplied the non-Catholic minorities in predominantly Catholic countries with a powerful

21

weapon for the defense of their freedom. The spirit which made the weapon possible will, in the long run, probably also make it unnecessary.

In other predominantly Christian countries the situation is generally better although by no means uniformly so. On the negative side, one could call attention to limitations of "proselytism" in Greece or to the tenuous position in Ethiopia of religious groups other than the Ethiopian Orthodox Church. In numerous Protestant and Eastern Orthodox countries the dominant church enjoys legal establishment. While this is not to be equated directly with religious persecution, it raises problems concerning religious liberty on a more subtle level. Marginal groups, such as Jehovah's Witnesses, may experience legal and practical difficulties even in countries like the United States where the governing principle is separation of church and state.

In predominantly Moslem countries, it is typical for Islam to be the legally established faith. Others, such as Christians and Hindus, often experience degrees of difficulty. An illustration would be the recent expulsion of a number of Eastern Orthodox leaders from Turkey. Some Moslem countries, such as Somaliland, guarantee freedom of worship but at the same time prohibit the open propagation of faiths other than Islam. Controversies between Moslems and adherents of other faiths have deep international significance in such situations as the India-Pakistan dispute, the conflict between Israel and the Arab countries, and the internal dissensions on the island of Cyprus.

In the non-Moslem Afro-Asian countries, which are generally Buddhist or Hindu, there are also problems. India, for example, while committed to religious liberty in principle and providing legal support for Christian religious activities, is notoriously reluctant to receive missionaries. Ceylon and Burma have established Buddhism as the state religion and thus aroused considerable apprehension among non-Buddhists. Conflicts between Buddhists and Catholics in South Vietnam have raised many issues of religious liberty and have immeasurably complicated an already chaotic revolutionary and military situation in that country. In many of the Afro-Asian countries, independence has been accompanied by a new nationalistic spirit in which religions associated with a former colonial era have been driven into a more precarious political situation. The legal establishment of Buddhism and Islam in some countries may owe a great deal to the assertion of the traditional religion against western cultural influences. In such situations, a traditional religion may serve as an important rallying point for nationalistic fervor and pride.

It is probable that in Communist countries religious liberty is most consistently denied. For various reasons it is difficult to gain an accurate perspective on this issue in Western countries. The truth is likely somewhere between the common Western impression of merciless religious persecution behind an "Iron Curtain" and the impression one would gain by reading the constitutions of Communist countries—which usually guarantee freedom of religious worship. Unquestionably Marxism is in such lands the officially established faith, and the Marxist attitude toward non-Marxist religions is one of hostility (this will be discussed more fully in the last chapter). This attitude has been implemented through various forms of official restrictions, such as denial of facilities for printing religious literature, exclusion from the public mass media, difficulties for Christian, Jewish, and Moslem students in continuing their education on the university level, denial of permission to Christian and Jewish groups to conduct

23

education for their young people, etc. Meanwhile the government, through channels of public school education and mass media, characteristically conducts an unrelenting campaign of opposition to religious "superstition."

Paradoxically, however, in several Communist countries church buildings, theological seminaries, and even the salaries of priests and ministers may largely be provided by the state (partly reflecting holdover patterns from pre-Communist times and partly reflecting public ownership of necessary facilities). Moreover, in a couple of instances religious groups are officially represented in national legislative bodies. Such support and recognition probably derives both from practical necessity in view of the large numbers of practicing Christians, Jews, and Moslems in Marxist lands, and from a desire to maintain a degree of control over the policies of religious groups as they affect the state. But despite such qualifications religious liberty remains a serious, unresolved problem in all Communist countries.

Religious persecution, then, is far from being a dead issue anywhere in the world. Even in such comparatively enlightened countries as the United States, Switzerland, Great Britain, and France there is a continuing challenge to understand and apply the idea of religious liberty with greater clarity. For even in such countries the relationship of religious groups to one another and to the state is so complex that issues of religious liberty and the proper relationship of church and state continue to vex political statesmanship and religious leadership alike.

An interesting illustration was provided by Switzerland in 1962 when the German theologian Helmut Gollwitzer was nominated to replace Karl Barth who was retiring from the chair of systematic theology at the University of Basel. Despite the fact that Gollwitzer had been properly designated by the Protestant theological faculty, the State Committee on Education refused to confirm the nomination, and the Basel Minister of Education proceeded to fill the vacant professorship with an alternate appointment. Notwithstanding his acknowledged stature as a theologian, Gollwitzer's appointment was vetoed because of the unpopularity of his political views. Theological standing was contravened by political authority on the basis of nontheological criteria in a nation which enjoys an enviable reputation as a sanctuary of freedom.

In the United States, issues of religious liberty have most recently appeared as a result of a series of Supreme Court decisions dealing with religion in public education. In the early 1960's the Court declared such religious practices as prayer and devotional Bible reading in the classroom to be unconstitutional. While the Court exempted the objective study of religious traditions, literature, and institutions from the effect of its rulings, the decisions have been greeted by a vast wave of protest. Many people saw in them a denial of religious liberty and the ominous threat of an emerging "godless" society. In 1964 a powerful effort was mounted to amend the Constitution by designating the United States as a Christian nation and by providing for due public recognition, in schools and elsewhere, of the supposed common faith of the American people. Although the movement failed, it demonstrated the great complexity which accompanies the application of religious liberty even in a society whose traditions seem committed to it. More significantly, it laid bare the deep divisions in American public opinion as to the underlying meaning of the traditional American slogans of religious liberty and separation of church and state and showed that religious liberty needs to be understood as both a very old and a very contemporary problem.

2. An Unconscious Commitment in Search of Basis

Even though religious liberty is far from being a reality in many parts of the world, and even though it may not be realized *perfectly* anywhere, one can still venture the assertion that it is one of those axiomatic commitments which are common to most of mankind. It is an important part of the *ius gentium* in the emerging world civilization. Despite religious intolerance and persecution, there is evidence that most people believe in freedom of religion and that the denial of religious liberty is everywhere on the defensive.

This is curiously evident in the fact that guarantees for freedom of worship are to be found in so many national constitutions—even in those of governments which are committed to viewpoints which seem irreconcilable with religious liberty. For instance, even the Soviet Constitution (in Article 124) states: "In order to guarantee to the citizens the freedom of conscience, the church in the USSR is separated from the state and the school is separated from the church; freedom for the performance of the religious rites and freedom of anti-religious propaganda are guaranteed to every citizen." That such provisions are ambiguous, that they may have been enacted through sheer expediency, or that they may be understood cynically does not change their importance. It is expedient to affirm at least some degree of freedom of worship because it is demanded by large numbers of people. Even cynicism in these matters is not to be discounted entirely, for it contains at least a silent tribute to a norm even though it may not genuinely accept commitment to it. Inclusion of freedom of worship as a constitutional provision bears public witness that there *ought* to be freedom in religious matters.

This commitment is even more manifest in the pronouncements of universal bodies which reflect the emerging world community. The United Nations, for instance, has since its inception affirmed religious liberty to be one of man's fundamental rights. At several points the Universal Declaration of Human Rights supports religious liberty indirectly. In Article 18 it forthrightly declares that "everyone has the right to freedom of thought, conscience and religion; this right includes freedom to change his religion or belief, and freedom, either alone or in community with others and in public or private, to manifest his religion or belief in teaching, practice, worship and observance." The United Nations Commission on Human Rights has continued to show the keenest interest in the subject. It currently has under discussion a draft of a wide-ranging "Declaration on the Elimination of all Forms of Religious Intolerance" which seeks to anticipate and condemn every possible kind of religious intolerance and persecution.[3]

The World Council of Churches has similarly given categorical support to religious liberty as a universal principle ever since the founding of that body in 1948. In a lengthy declaration the Amsterdam Asssembly of the World Council, which was held in that year, carefully analyzed the meaning of religious liberty and asserted that "the rights of religious freedom herein declared shall be recognized and observed for all persons without distinction as to race, colour, sex, language, or religion, and without imposition of disability by virtue of legal provision or administrative acts." [4]

As suggested above, it is also of the greatest significance that the Vatican Council has committed Roman Catholicism in a declaration supporting religious liberty. No matter how one may wish to criticize this declaration, strong movement in this direction by so vast and worldwide a religious community is profoundly important. The fact that Catholicism has often been associated with the denial of religious liberty only underscores this as evidence of an emerging worldwide consensus of the human community concerning the rightness of the principle. Significantly, the Declaration itself places great stress upon the "growing consciousness" of mankind that man must enjoy freedom if he is to be fully human, and that this "is particularly applicable in matters of religion." Both the Declaration and its principal architect, Father John Courtney Murray, strongly suggest that it is precisely the emerging human consciousness of the importance of freedom which has made it possible for the church to affirm religious liberty and still be true to its own nature. More will need to be said about the Declaration later. Here I am simply suggesting that its form and adoption are a kind of crowning evidence of the near-universal commitment to religious liberty which is emerging.

But despite this general commitment, there is by no means a universal consensus as to *why* there should be religious liberty. I have referred to the commitment as an "unconscious" one. This is not to say that people are committed to the idea without being aware of it, which would be absurd. But it is to say that people are committed to the idea without having consciously grounded it in relation to other things they believe. Indeed, it is probable that many people believe in religious liberty *in spite of* their other beliefs. Among the friends of religious liberty there are to be found adherents of groups which are exclusivistic, intolerant, and even arrogant. This is splendid witness to the contemporary power of the idea and to the universality of commitment to it. But it also suggests danger.

In the first place, it raises the question *why* we are supporting this principle. Is it really only because we find it expedient at the present time? Is it because we have already rejected elements in our own less tolerant traditions and that religious liberty now represents a more fundamental faith for some unknown reason? What will happen when there is a direct conflict between the two commitments—as when our religious group gains overwhelming social and political power and ventures to use that power against others?

In the second place, it raises the question *how far* we would be willing to apply religious liberty as a principle. Until we know the basis of the principle, the manner and extent of its application must remain uncertain. It may remain the kind of popular slogan which can mean one thing to one person but quite a different thing to others.

In the third place, it raises the question of the extent to which persons of different faiths can trust one another with respect to a common commitment to this principle.

There is little ground for hope that reflection about the basis of the principle will result in a universal consensus. Anticipating later discussion, it is possible that a kind of natural-law understanding based upon the common sense of mankind will be able to develop into a consensus. It is my hope that the idea of a responsible state might serve in this way (cf. chap V). But so long as there are religious differences, persons reflecting such differences will need to come to grips with religious liberty *in terms of the deepest insight of their own traditions*. While this in itself will not yield a consensus (short of the unlikely future merging of all religious faiths or the conversion of everybody to any one faith), it can at least lead to communication and a form of reassurance. To illustrate, I am not a Marxist and the prospect of my becoming a Marxist is remote. But as a non-Marxist who must live in the same world with Marxists I would be reassured if good Marxist theoreticians could find convincing support for religious liberty at the center of their doctrine, and if this fresh interpretation of Marxism were to become accepted generally throughout the Communist movement. I would similarly be reassured by such support coming from the center of Buddhist, Moslem, and Hindu religious thought. And I assume that persons of such faiths would, in turn, be pleased to discover that Protestant and Catholic Christians and adherents of the various Jewish traditions find support for religious liberty at the center of their theologies. While this effort may never produce a universal consensus as to the religious basis for religious liberty, it cannot fail to promote greater security for the idea and greater clarity in its political application.

For the present, however, it must be said merely that the search for the most profound basis for religious liberty is on. The fate of the principle ultimately depends upon that search. If the age-old problem of religious persecution and coercion is to be abolished in our time, it will largely be because the principle of religious liberty has become grounded in the central beliefs and values of mankind.

3. The Roman Catholic Position and Dilemma

Nowhere is this search more strikingly visible than in the Roman Catholic Church. For the past generation a creative group of Catholic scholars in Europe and America has diligently sought to ground religious liberty in Catholic doctrine.[5] These scholars have not all been agreed as to the most fruitful direction to pursue.[6] But they have in common a commitment to religious liberty which is deep and principled as to its rightness in Roman Catholic perspective. Their labor was largely responsible for the adoption of the Declaration on Religious Liberty by the fourth session of the Second Vatican Council.

This movement is interesting for its stark contrast to traditional Roman Catholic teaching and practice. Indeed, one of its most demanding tasks has been to demonstrate that much previous Roman Catholic teaching is not as authoritative as many have supposed. This has not been easy, for an impressive number of authoritative papal encyclicals can be marshaled in support of the suppression of non-Catholic religious views by a Roman Catholic state. For example, in his encyclical *Libertae Praestantissimum* Pope Leo XIII declared that

Men have a right freely and prudently to propagate throughout the State what things soever are true and honorable, so that as many as possible may possess them; but lying opinions . . . should be diligently repressed by public authority, lest they insidiously work the ruin of the State. The excesses of an unbridled intellect, which unfailingly end in the oppression of the untutored multitude, are no less rightly controlled by the authority of the law than are the injuries inflicted by violence upon the weak.

In his various encyclicals this same pope made clear that the best possible situation would be one in which the Roman Catholic Church would alone enjoy the recognition and material support of the state while other religious views would be repressed or at least discouraged. In situations where the state was not controlled by Roman Catholics or where the size and variety of other religious groups made repression or too great favoritism for Roman Catholicism impracticable, religious freedom and the separation of church and state could be embraced in good conscience. It was made clear, however, that this was by way of concession to undesirable circumstances for the sake of the public good.

The more traditional Catholic theory has held that, since rights are grounded in man's freedom to obey God, there cannot be an objective right to act in opposition to God. Cardinal Alfredo Ottaviani, one of the best known and most articulate contemporary supporters of the traditionalist position, argued that such rights as freedom of religion,

have very well as their subjects those individuals who find themselves in possession of the truth; and that other individuals cannot demand the same rights by title of the error they profess. . . . The first Subject of these rights is God Himself. From this it follows that only they who obey His commands and who possess His truth and His justice have true rights.[7]

Thus, it has been argued that when Catholicism is in the possession of political power it should use that power to deny freedom to other groups. Only when Catholicism does not have this power should it affirm the freedom of competing forms of religion. This theory has generally been related to the distinction between "thesis" and "hypothesis," the former indicating the ideal situation, the latter reflecting deviations from the ideal rendered necessary or desirable by adverse historical circumstances. A. F. Carrillo de Albornoz has accurately summarized the position:

In "thesis," that is to say when pure Roman Catholic principles can be applied, "error" must not be free to propagate or to be propagated. Only in the "hypothesis," namely, when owing to adverse circumstances, Roman Catholics cannot prudently impose their principles, can freedom of "error" be provisionally tolerated *as the lesser evil.*[8]

It is a tribute both to the new leadership and to the spirit of the times that more liberal Catholic leadership should succeed in leading the church away from this conception of orthodoxy in one generation. Without discarding the basic assumption that the Catholic Church is indeed in possession of the fullness of truth and means of salvation and that other groups are relatively in error, the newer view has argued that religious liberty is a right which is grounded in men rather than in truth as such. The theological and juridical basis of the human right has been argued differently by different theologians. But common to most of them is a conception of the dignity of man as God's creature which applies despite man's error. Characteristic also is the idea that religious faith is something which, by definition, cannot be imposed through force. This newer view is committed to the application of religious liberty even in countries where the Roman Catholic Church is dominant. Its argument is further that this position does not make a radical break with Catholic tradition, a point which possibly must be made if the claim that Catholicism is the one true church of Christ is not to be undercut through conceding errors of past teachings. Continuity with tradition is preserved in two basic ways. First, it is indicated that all previous teaching on religious liberty which is inconsistent with the newer view was intended to apply to specific historical situations which are now past. Furthermore, liberal or democratic ideas which were previously condemned—such as in the famous "Syllabus of Errors" of Pope Pius IX—were themselves not in the context of contemporary democracy but in the context of the totalitarian pretensions and anti-clericalism of European, particularly French, rationalists. In other words, truth was relevantly applied by such popes as Pius IX and Leo XIII, both of whom *seem* to have opposed the principle of religious liberty. But truth applied relevantly today demands an entirely different stance: it requires a principled support for religious liberty. Time may indeed make ancient good appear uncouth; but this is because of changing conditions, not because the church is becoming more faithful to truth than she was in the past. A second way in which continuity with tradition may be preserved, which may be understood as a variation of the first, has been proposed by the eminent Jesuit theologian Fr. John Courtney Murray. The contention is that the decisive change in conditions is the growing world consciousness of the exigency of religious liberty. As Fr. Murray has put it,

The common consciousness of men today considers the demand for personal, social, and political freedom to be an exigency that rises from the depths of the human person. It is the expression of a sense of right approved by reason. It is therefore a demand of natural law in the present moment of history.

Therefore, he continues,

in consequence of the new perspective created by the growth of the personal and political consciousness, the state of the ancient question concerning public care of religion has been altered. . . . The terms of the argument today are, quite simply, religious freedom. The question is to know, first, what religious freedom means in the common consciousness today, and second, why religious freedom, in the sense of the common consciousness, is to receive the authoritative approval of the Church.[9]

The problem, then, is not to find a static ideal which would impose the same political solution on every era in spite of concrete conditions and states of mind; the problem rather is to be responsive to the dynamic changes of history and to search out from the church's teachings the true and relevant response to new conditions and forms of consciousness. In our era this requires affirming a prin-

34

cipled (that is, nonexpedient) policy of religious liberty even for those countries in which Catholicism is politically most powerful.

When one turns to the Declaration on Religious Liberty adopted by the ecumenical Council in 1965, the influence of such thoughts is readily apparent. At the same time, the Declaration as a product of the Council's deliberative process is somewhat more eclectic than the writings of such a thinker as Fr. Murray. The significance of the Declaration rests not simply on its intrinsic merits or obvious meanings, but quite as much upon the way in which it is to be applied and interpreted. Time alone will reveal its full importance, although one can already suggest that it presents to the world a fundamentally new Catholic orientation on religious liberty. There is no precedent in definitive Catholic literature for a statement such as the following:

This Vatican Synod declares that the human person has a right to religious freedom. This freedom means that all men are to be immune from coercion on the part of individuals or of social groups and of any human power, in such wise that no one is to be forced to act in a manner contrary to his own beliefs, whether privately or publicly, whether alone or in association with others, within due limits.

The Synod further declares that the right to religious freedom has its foundation in the very dignity of the human person as this dignity is known through the revealed word of God and by reason itself. This right of the human person to religious freedom is to be recognized in the constitutional law whereby society is governed. Thus it is to become a civil right.[10]

The seriousness of this statement is underscored by the concreteness with which it is applied. Two or three sentences will illustrate this. For example, it says that religious communities also have the right not to be hindered, either by legal measures or by administrative action on the part of government, in the selection, training, appointment, and transferral of their own ministers, in communicating with religious authorities and communities abroad, in erecting buildings for religious purposes, and in the acquisition and use of suitable funds or properties.

In another paragraph, it is made clear that "religious communities also have the right not to be hindered in their public teaching and witness to their faith, whether by the spoken or by the written word."

And, as a final illustration,

religious communities should not be prohibited from freely undertaking to show the special value of their doctrine in what concerns the organization of society and the inspiration of the whole of human activity.

The possible *uses* of such statements, both within and beyond the Catholic Church, are obviously numerous— regardless of the theological rationale or limiting qualifications. For this reason it may seem gratuitous to examine the Declaration further.

It is, however, necessary to ask whether and to what extent the Declaration could supply continuing justification for the maintenance of the *status quo* in Spain and some of the other predominantly Roman Catholic countries where religious liberty has been a problem for non-Catholics. From this perspective, some of the qualifying limitations placed upon religious liberty may prove troublesome. For example, in one of the paragraphs quoted above religious freedom means immunity from coercion "within due limits." What did the Synod mean by "due limits"? Clearly it was not desirous of creating a loophole for the abuse of religious freedom, for it is stated that "government is not to act in an arbitrary fashion or in an unfair spirit of partisanship." Rather, "its action is to be controlled by juridical norms which are in conformity with the objective moral order." Such norms are held to

arise out of the need for the effective safeguard of the rights of all citizens and for the peaceful settlement of conflicts of rights, also out of the need for an adequate care of genuine public peace, which comes about when men live together in good order and in true justice, and finally out of the need for a proper guardianship of public morality.

It is further held that "the freedom of man is to be respected as far as possible and is not to be curtailed except when and insofar as necessary."

As I have suggested, the *intent* of this seems clear enough. But the language introduces principles of limitation of freedom which are subject to broad interpretation —particularly when one reflects that the Catholic Church has sometimes held views of "the objective moral order" with which most other persons have been in disagreement. For example, would advocacy of the responsibilities of planned parenthood and encouragement of the use of contraceptive devices be considered consistent with "public morality" as understood in relation to "the objective moral order"? Would non-Catholic public preaching be construed as a disturbance of the peace in a predominantly Roman Catholic society? The difficulty, again, may not lie so much with the intent of the Declaration as with the latitude of interpretation which it permits.

An additional problem is raised by the schema in the

specific provision which is made for particular religious groups to be given preferential treatment under certain circumstances, provided that there is no interference with the religious liberty of other groups and individuals. This is stated as follows:

If, in view of peculiar circumstances obtaining among peoples, special civil recognition is given to one religious community in the constitutional order of society, it is at the same time imperative that the right of all citizens and religious communities to religious freedom should be recognized and made effective in practice.

I mention this point here because it will be necessary later to raise the question whether religious establishment is really consistent with religious liberty.

There is one final point of emphasis in the Declaration which may have important ultimate implications for the Roman Catholic stance on religious liberty. That is the careful statement that the Declaration "leaves untouched traditional Catholic doctrine on the moral duty of men and societies toward the true religion and toward the one Church of Christ." That this latter is to be understood as the Catholic Church is underscored by the statement that

God himself has made known to mankind the way in which men are to serve him, and thus be saved in Christ and come to blessedness. We believe that this one true religion subsists in the catholic and apostolic church, to which the Lord Jesus committed the duty of spreading it abroad among all men.

This point was emphasized in Council debate. For example, at one point after the Declaration draft had been accepted in principle, the Council fathers voted affirmatively on the addition of the following words: "Since all men are bound to search for truth especially in those things which concern the worship of God (religion) and to serve it, they are bound by sacred duty to profess and embrace the Catholic faith insofar as they are able to know it." [11] Concurrently it was reemphasized that religious liberty should not be construed as freedom to question the authoritative teaching of the church.

A distinction must of course be made between the internal discipline of a religious group and political religious liberty, provided that a person is free to leave the religious group without political hindrances or consequences. But the Catholic Church may nevertheless face a real dilemma because of its exclusive and absolute claims. While there is no reason to doubt the sincerity of the new generation of Catholic political thinkers or the good faith of the church in adopting its basically progressive Declaration on Religious Liberty, it may yet be said that the basis still remains upon which the older claims of dogmatic intolerance were previously made. I am thinking of the claim that the Catholic Church is the repository of absolute religious truth and objectively valid means of grace, in relation to which other religious claims are relatively in error, and of the hierarchical system which remains for the authoritative interpretation of doctrine.

One is reminded here of Ernst Troeltsch's account of the failure of the conciliar movement in the late Middle Ages. The conciliar movement attempted to broaden ecclesiastical power from the papacy to the bishops and priests, with some possibilities for lay participation. According to Troeltsch, the movement failed "since it could not even imagine in theory the abolition of the real root of the institutional conception in priesthood, sacrament and hierarchy." [12] The logic of objective sacramental grace is centralization rather than broad distribution of power. Similarly, if modern Catholicism is still understood to possess infallibility in dogma and objective means of grace, identified with institutional forms and administered by an authoritative priesthood and hierarchy, does there not remain a logical basis for political efforts to further the church in its *objectively valid* mission and to impede competitive efforts insofar as circumstances of time and place permit? Has the new conciliar movement really destroyed in principle the old theory of thesis-hypothesis? To put the question in a different way, has the Declaration on Religious Liberty been developed *in spite of* Catholicism's doctrine of the Church? And, if so, is there the possibility that at some future time other Catholic thinkers may prefer to base their approach to religious liberty once more on the absolute and exclusive doctrine of the Church? One may believe the question to be largely academic in the present spirit of ecumenicity, but at the same time one may continue to hope for further modifications of the doctrine of the Church.

The judgment must therefore be ventured that, despite the splendid work which a generation of liberal Catholic scholars has effected, much more thought must still be given to the basis in Christian theology of religious liberty. In particular, Catholic scholars will need to do more thinking about the precise relationship between Catholic views of infallibility and authority on the one hand, and the whole question of religious liberty on the other.

While the present work is concerned with the Protestant perspective, some of the "inadequate foundations" discussed in the second chapter correspond to bases upon which Roman Catholic scholars have occasionally sought to ground religious liberty. For this reason I shall in that context occasionally mention the work of such writers. But the theological foundation upon which I have myself sought to base religious liberty is one which is specifically inconsistent with Catholic claims of infallibility and authority as I understand them. I hope that the present work may help to stimulate further Catholic reflection and resolve what I suggested to be the dilemma of the Catholic position.

4. New Protestant Ambiguities

If Catholicism is wrestling with the question of religious liberty in a fresh and creative way, it is not merely catching up with Protestant insight. It may be safe to say that *American* Protestantism has generally been committed to the principle. But Catholics can testify to rugged experiences in predominantly Protestant lands where Protestants have had the power of establishment. One thinks of Cromwell's classic statement to the Irish Catholics concerning religious liberty: "As to freedom of conscience, I meddle with no man's conscience; but if you mean by that, liberty to celebrate the Mass, I would have you understand that in no place where the power of the Parliament of England prevails shall that be permitted." [13] Moreover, historic Protestantism has often enough articulated theories in support of religious persecution. This has been true of much continental Protestantism until the recent past. Even in America the Protestant tendency has been to ground its ideas in American democratic political traditions as an alternative for theological reflection, and it must not be overlooked that American Protestant practice, when it has embraced nativism, has been anything but sensitive to the rights of Catholics and others.

We Protestants are becoming aware in new ways that far too little attention has ever been given to the theological basis of our understanding of religious liberty. In America this is evident in the confusion which has re-

41

sulted from the recent Supreme Court decisions affecting religion and the schools. In the 1960's American Protestants have suddenly awakened to the realization that they really have no common doctrine of religious liberty and church-state relations on whose basis they might approach the more complex current issues. Professor Thomas G. Sanders has clarified the reasons for this lack.[14] He located and analyzed no fewer than five major Protestant traditions on church-state relations. The increased expression of these different traditions has added to a sense of ambiguity of the overall Protestant witness.

Added to this ambiguity has been the fact that two groups, which sometimes espouse conflicting viewpoints, have sought to formulate and register Protestant opinion on church-state matters. One group, Protestants and Other Americans United for Separation of Church and State (POAU), has emerged since World War II reflecting a more absolute conception of the separation of church and state. It has more typically based its views on American tradition than upon theological reflection. Its influence is great and it unquestionably reflects the support of millions of American Protestants. The other group is the National Council of the Churches of Christ in the U.S.A., with its increasingly active Commission on Religious Liberty. While the National Council with its predecessor, the Federal Council of Churches, has represented American Protestantism for more than half a century, its leadership in the field of religious liberty is much more recent. Increasingly, however, it is recognized as the most authentic voice of American Protestantism and Eastern Orthodoxy in this field, and its constituency considerably overlaps that of POAU.

A significant National Study Conference on Church and State, which was sponsored by the National Council's De-

partment of Religious Liberty in 1964, made the conflicts and ambiguities of American Protestant witness
abundantly clear to most observers.[15] This was particularly
apparent in the attempts to get at the theological basis of
religious liberty. While the conference made numerous
contributions to ongoing Protestant thought, it clearly revealed that there is no consensus among contemporary
American Protestants as to precisely *why* religious liberty
is an important commitment—even though it did reveal
that most Protestants are committed to the principle.

5. The Opportunity for New Protestant Witness

The present world cultural situation may have presented
Protestant Christians with an unparalleled opportunity to
witness effectively to their principled support for religious
liberty. I write this on the assumption that there can be
such a witness, for I am convinced that there is at the heart
of Protestant Christian faith a profound basis for this idea
which now claims the unconscious support of so large a
part of mankind.

In this situation, Protestant Christians are particularly
challenged to demonstrate that the cultural successes of
Protestant Christianity need be feared by no friend of religious liberty whether or not he is a Christian. To bear
this kind of witness, it is not necessary for Protestants to
convert others to Protestantism. It is only necessary to
show the logical connection between Protestant faith as
such and the principle of religious liberty.

In his approach to this problem, the Protestant must
avoid the temptation of making religious liberty his prior
commitment. Presumably the Protestant Christian is Christian first. Religious liberty follows, it does not precede, his
commitment to the Christian faith. To say this is not to be
arrogant. It is simply to remember that religious liberty is

a principle to organize social policy; it is not a religious faith in and of itself. But such principles may be rooted finally in religious faith assumptions. The Protestant Christian must do justice to his deepest faith assumptions if he is to do justice to the principle. It is, however, both legitimate and necessary to let the issue of religious liberty seek rationalization or grounding in Christian theology, provided the rationalization does not distort the meaning of Christian faith—that is, provided that the rationalization is at the same time authentic Christian rationale. Religious liberty as a commitment and as a problem raises questions which are directed toward every religious faith, including that of the Protestant Christian.

In the following chapters I intend to explore first the bases which have been advanced in support of religious liberty but must be considered inadequate. In succeeding chapters I shall outline a negative and positive theological support for religious liberty and a theory of the responsible state. Finally, I shall suggest various avenues of application and some possibilities for future dialogue between Protestants and others.

NOTES

[1] Francesco Ruffini, *Religious Libetry* (New York: G. P. Putnam's Sons, 1912, tr. J. Parker Heyes), p. 18.

[2] This discussion is particularly indebted to Angel F. Carrillo de Albornoz, *Religious Liberty: A General Review of the Present Situation in the World* (Geneva: World Council of Churches, 1964). Current developments, particularly in the United States, are surveyed in the quarterly *A Journal of Church and State* and the annual review *Religion and the Public Order*. The constantly evolving religious situation in Marxist lands is chronicled in the semimonthly bulletin *Religion in Communist Dominated Areas*, which is published by the International Affairs Commission of the National Council of Churches in the United States. The rapid pace of contemporary developments respecting religious liberty is clearly

manifest when one refers again to M. Searle Bates's excellent world survey of twenty years ago in *Religious Liberty: An Inquiry* (New York: Harper and Brothers, 1945).

[3] The very difficulty of anticipating every possible problem of religious liberty has led a commission of the World Council of Churches to suggest that it might be preferable to restrict the Declaration to general principles which would be categorical and inclusive. If some specific abuses are singled out for condemnation, it is possible to interpret the omission of other abuses as acceptance of their legitimacy. Cf. Carrillo, *Religious Liberty*, pp. 28-34.

[4] World Council of Churches, *The Church and the International Disorder* (New York: Harper and Brothers, 1948). The passage cited is in the Report of Section IV at p. 226.

[5] A. F. Carrillo de Albornoz, *Roman Catholicism and Religious Liberty* (Geneva: World Council of Churches, 1959), is the most widely accepted introduction to this movement, even though it is the work of a Protestant scholar. See also John Courtney Murray, S. J., *The Problem of Religious Freedom* (Westminster, Md.: The Newman Press, 1965) and Eric D'Arcy, *Conscience and Its Right to Freedom* (New York: Sheed and Ward, 1961), two recent contributions by significant figures in this movement. Murray's thought is ably discussed and criticized by Thomas T. Love, *John Courtney Murray: Contemporary Church-State Theory* (Garden City, N.Y.: Doubleday, 1965).

[6] There is a tendency among European Catholic scholars favorable to religious liberty to seek a distinctively theological basis for the principle, while American scholars, largely following Murray, tend to prefer a juridical approach. Unresolved differences between these two orientations apparently contributed to delay in adoption of the Declaration on Religious Liberty at the Vatican Council.

[7] Quoted by Joseph J. Baierl, *The Catholic Church and the Modern State* (Rochester, N.Y.: St. Bernard's Seminary, 1955), p. 223. The passage is from a speech delivered by the cardinal in 1953.

[8] *Roman Catholicism and Religious Liberty*, p. 5.

[9] *The Problem of Religious Freedom*, pp. 18-19.

[10] Quotations from Vatican Council Declarations used in the present work are from *The Documents of Vatican II* (New York: Guild Press, The America Press, and Association Press, 1966). Used by permission.

[11] As quoted by United Press International, Oct. 26, 1965.

[12] Ernst Troeltsch, *The Social Teaching of the Christian Churches* (New York: The Macmillan Co., 1931 [1911]), I, 376.

[13] Quoted by Sidney Hook, *The Paradoxes of Freedom* (Berkeley and Los Angeles: University of California Press, 1962), p. 23.

[14] *Protestant Concepts of Church and State* (New York: Holt, Rinehart and Winston, 1964).

[15] My own interpretation of the Conference appears in the article "The NCC National Study Conference on Church and State" in the 1964 volume of *Religion and the Public Order* (Chicago: University of Chicago Press, 1965), pp. 121-48.

II

Inadequate Foundations

The task of supplying intellectual foundation for the principle of religious liberty is, as we have said, an important one if the principle is to be sustained and wisely applied in the religious and ideological crossfire of contemporary times. The task has enlisted an army of thinkers in this and previous generations, and the diversity of their proposals can be bewildering. The present book, too, has a point of view to advance. But first it is necessary to examine several important lines of approach which have found wide acceptance but which seem to provide inadequate support for the principle. In this chapter I shall examine five approaches of current significance. Three of these are based on general (nontheological) grounds. The other two rest upon Christian theological insight. While no attempt can be made here to examine the full subtlety with which these positions have sometimes been presented, I have sought to capture their essential possibilities and to provide essential criticism. Despite the designation of each of these views as an "inadequate foundation," each undoubtedly has an important contribution to make.

1. National Tradition and Constitutional Authority

In the United States it is common for discussion of religious liberty and church-state relations to be grounded in the generally accepted national traditions of freedom and separation of church and state. To a striking degree the national tradition itself, particularly as it is embodied in the Constitution, has become a kind of final normative source of authority. This American tendency is not merely provincial. The United States has had unique experience as a laboratory for the testing of religious liberty, and American traditions consequently have had influence far beyond these shores.

It is interesting that Fr. John Courtney Murray should choose to organize his important book on church and state [1] in terms of "Catholic reflections on the American proposition," even though he makes it clear that to him the fundamental issue is not whether Catholicism is adequate as a foundation for American traditions of church and state but whether a Catholic can in conscience accept those traditions. More direct appeal is often made by Protestant, Jewish, and secularist authors. Appeal to national tradition and constitutional norms is often embodied in the official statements of denominational groups and the National Council of Churches, which habitually supports conclusions in church-state areas at least partly on constitutional grounds.

Perhaps the clearest illustration of this approach is pro-

vided by Protestants and Other Americans United for
Separation of Church and State (POAU), which was until
very recently the dominant voice of American Protestantism on church-state issues. POAU has rooted its position
of strict separation and absolute religious liberty on its
conception of American tradition and the U.S. Constitution. In the Manifesto which it issued at its founding in
1947, it declared,

Its single and only purpose is to assure the maintenance of
the American principle of separation of church and state
upon which the Federal Constitution guarantees religious
liberty to all the people and all churches of this Republic.
PROTESTANTS AND OTHER AMERICANS UNITED
has been called into existence because this principle has been
and is being violated, and threatened with further violation,
in certain areas and by certain acts of both government and
church. The plain meaning of the First Amendment to the
Constitution, which forbids Congress to make any law "respecting an establishment of religion" has been obscured by
specious propaganda tending to confuse the public mind as
to the clear-cut line of separation which this Amendment
draws between church and state. We shall endeavor (1) to
revive in the public mind a clear understanding of the constitutional basis upon which religious liberty has been guaranteed, (2) to redress the specific violations which have recently
come into force, and (3) to resist further encroachments upon
this constitutional principle.[2]

While POAU leadership occasionally discusses the question *why* the American tradition is basically sound, the
authority to which it most typically appeals is that tradition itself.

What is the American tradition? As it has been reflected
in numerous writings, in the instinctive responses of the
"man on the street," and in dicta of the Supreme Court,

49

the tradition flatly affirms the absolute separation of church and state (frequently employing Jefferson's phrase, "wall of separation between Church and State," and sometimes mistakenly considering it a part of the Constitution) and the complementary principle of religious liberty. These principles are considered to reflect essential insights of the "founding fathers" of the nation, and are thus invested with all the sanctity which attaches to the basis of community life and patriotism. It was, it is held, for the sake of such essentials that the fathers established a new nation despite many sacrifices and much struggle. In their wisdom, these essentials were carefully included in the Bill of Rights and were adhered to generally throughout the early years of the republic. It has been the task of subsequent generations to preserve and defend these principles against open attack or subtle erosion. Organizations like POAU see their *raison d'être* in precisely such terms, and in many of its dicta (particularly in the majority decision rendered by Mr. Justice Black in the Everson case) the Supreme Court likewise has interpreted its role. Often those who have been most sensitive to encroachments of the "wall of separation" have seen those encroachments as emanating from Roman Catholicism. Thus, for example, Roman Catholic candidates for public office, such as Al Smith and John F. Kennedy, have been subjected to the most exacting scrutiny as to the effect their election might have upon preservation of the tradition.

American national tradition, indeed, is not to be despised by any lover of religious liberty, for commitment to that principle has run deep here. Simple reliance upon that tradition as a source of authority poses numerous problems, however.

In the first place, as Franklin H. Littell has demonstrated, the tradition itself is more complex than generally supposed.[3] Residues from the older colonial establishments of religion, especially in Massachusetts, Connecticut, and Virginia, persisted well into the nineteenth century. The principle of separation was not systematically applied to the states until after the Civil War and the adoption of the Fourteenth Amendment, which made the Bill of Rights applicable to actions of the state governments. Moreover, even such exemplars of the tradition as Jefferson and Madison did not consistently support it—at least not in the absolutist sense. Littell points out, for instance, that even Jefferson required regular attendance at Protestant chapel services when he was rector of the state-supported University of Virginia. On the basis of such facts Littell has argued that religious liberty is something we have never really had in any full sense of the term in this country. Protestant infringements upon the religious liberties of others, both subtle and overt, were easily overlooked by Protestants who could take their own point of view more or less for granted. Religious liberty therefore is conceived as something to be gone out for. Littell's historical opinion is the more impressive in light of his own deep commitment to the voluntary principle in religion, a principle which he derives, however, from theological grounds.[4] His perspective partly influenced the NCC Study Conference on Church and State of 1964, which stated that

the nation which adopted the First Amendment, at the same time considered itself both Christian and Protestant and saw no contradiction in passing laws which required Sunday observance, prayer and Bible reading in the public schools. Its actions attested to historical interaction as well as to separation of church and state.[5]

In the second place, reliance upon American tradition is uncertain because of the vast historical changes which have occurred in the brief history of this country. Uncritical absolutizing of the tradition, even when complexities attending its origin can be taken into account, runs afoul of the cultural differences between its application in the simple frontier conditions of early American life and the massive, highly complicated urban civilization of today.[6] Separation of church and state could more readily be maintained in a society in which both were relatively undeveloped. But, as the role of modern government has expanded in response to the needs of urban industrial society and as the churches have proliferated new forms of ministry in response to changing conditions, the traditions have been more and more difficult to apply in their absolute form. For instance, one must consider that all the following fields of complexity have emerged substantially *since* the origins of our national traditions governing relations of church and state:

a) government and church welfare,

b) public school education,

c) governmental research,

d) global commitments of government to military and economic assistance programs, which are paralleled by

e) international church missionary and welfare activities,

f) the development in this country of parochial school education, by the Roman Catholic Church,

g) governmental regulation of mass media of communications, particularly in the fields of radio and television, and

h) much more complicated forms of governmental taxation.

All this does not necessarily point away from the traditions, but it does suggest reexamination in the light of what is essential to those traditions. And to approach this task, a foundation more fundamental than the traditions themselves is needed as authority.

In the third place, there is the problem of relating religious liberty to separation of church and state as twin principles. More will be said about this problem later, for it is a key issue. But it must be said here that if both are made into absolutes serious contradictions can result. For instance, separation of church and state could mean that rapid expansions in the role of government serve as a wedge sweeping the cultural expressions of religion aside as government penetrates further and further into the life of the community in response to broader definitions of social justice. There may be an element of justification in the fears of some that separation of church and state, by creating a secular society, subtly plays havoc with religious liberty; although it must be added immediately that many such expressions of fear have come from those who sought to impose acceptance of their own particular faith as an alternative to secularism. Recognizing possible contradictions between the first two propositions of the First Amendment, a number of writers have wisely considered separation to be instrumental to religious liberty, with the interests of religious liberty regulating exceptions to separation rather than the reverse.

The need calls for deeper analysis than simple adherence to national tradition or constitutional authority as such can afford, important as tradition and authority are in expressing the consensus of this society.

2. Pluralism and Social Peace

We have already taken note of the importance of religious pluralism in the new dialogue on religious liberty. A whole school of thought today draws important conclusions from this in support of religious liberty and in interpretation of the non-establishment clause of the First Amendment. Symbolic of this is the fact that the term "pluralism" has assumed such prominence in most contemporary books on religion in America and in the pronouncements of most religious bodies on issues of church and state. The term "pluralism" has, in fact, been invoked so routinely in current discussion as to risk becoming a mere cliché. It reflects realities, however, which must be understood carefully in the context of religious liberty.

First of all, a strong case can be made that the institutionalization of religious liberty and the non-establishment of religion owe more to religious conflict than anything else. The great religious wars sapped the vitality of Europe and were revolting to men of sensitivity, whatever their particular religious alignments. If for no other reason, religious liberty was preferable to incessant conflict. It is worth remembering that England, the most important source of American traditions, was convulsed by religious conflict throughout the seventeenth century, the period which produced landmark thought in support of religious liberty and the beginnings of those institutions which were to find fruition in the American Bill of Rights a century later. America, of course, had religious diversity and conflict all its own. While religious intolerance and religious establishment were not unknown in America, their practical results were shabby enough in many respects to suggest the value of alternatives to the pragmatists who founded this nation.

Secondly, it is indeed relevant here that pluralism has matured in contemporary America into an even greater diversity. Professor Robert T. Handy has distinguished between the "Protestant pluralism" characteristic of seventeenth- and eighteenth-century America and the "radical pluralism" of the present.[7] During the former period, the culture was essentially Protestant, and religious pluralism primarily reflected differences internal to Protestantism. In the present day, however, Roman Catholicism has to be considered as a substantial element, along with Judaism and the whole range of religious viewpoints arising outside the Hebrew-Christian tradition.

The "radical pluralism" of the present is intensified by the incredibly rapid growth of communication between cultures through the mass media and vastly improved transportation which now places ranges of diversity in the immediate presence of even the most tightly secluded religious ghetto. American pluralism, diverse and distinct as its groupings have seemed, is relatively homogeneous when viewed in world perspective. Yet, through television and radio and the exchange of literature, students, and tourists, one can no longer ignore religions and cultures which are radically different.

Martin E. Marty and others have made much of the implications of this fact for the churches. No longer is it possible for persons anywhere simply to assume the truth of their worldview or cause. Only the most sheltered can avoid the fact that others see things differently. This means that all religious groups must face new forms of subtle and overt competition. More hopefully, it also means that they can escape some of the enervating effects of complacency. Vitality can be a by-product of pluralism. In this setting, however, it becomes even more unthinkable that religious repression should occur anywhere. Nor is it possible to *hide* religious repression anywhere. Spain may be homogeneous enough to indulge in the persecution of Protestants, for example, but Spain does not exist in isolation. What it does to its own Protestants affects Protestants and even Catholics everywhere. The same could be said of Protestant treatment of Catholics in Eire, or Communist treatment of Christians in Russia, or Christian treatment of Communists in America, and so on. The diverse groups of the world are entering into a new age of dialogue. While many people undoubtedly are not ready for dialogue, freedom of expression is unquestionably necessary for it to begin. It is therefore understandable that freedom is increasingly demanded by persons of every persuasion and culture.

So far as America is concerned, pluralism has had profound effect in defining the culture. According to Will Herberg, who may overstate the matter a bit, "religious pluralism is thus not merely a historical and political fact; it is, in the mind of the American, the primordial condition of things, an essential aspect of the American Way of Life, and therefore in itself an aspect of religious belief." [8] The political effect of this belief is the conviction "that the government may not do anything that implies the preeminence or superior legitimacy of one church over another." Conditioned thus by the great melting pot, Americans of all faiths have come to consider religious liberty an article of faith in and of itself—when in fact it has derived more from their common social experience of diversity.

It is not surprising that some, who see these implications of pluralism and who are skeptical of the persuasiveness of other bases of religious liberty, have argued that the surest foundation for the principle lies in the fact that it is simply good law. It preserves the peace and makes it possible for all groups to get along with their main business and, if they are so minded, with the dialogue.

The American Jesuit theologian John Courtney Murray, who makes a great deal of this view, is one of its ablest exponents. Murray distinguishes between articles of faith and articles of peace. The former are theologically necessary and have a sanctity derived from their religious content. The latter "are not invested with the sanctity that attaches to dogma, but only with the rationality that attaches to law." Arguing that freedom of religion and the nonestablishment clause of the First Amendment are articles of peace, Murray emphatically disagrees with "those who read into them certain ultimate beliefs, certain specifically sectarian tenets with regard to the nature of religion, religious truth, the church, faith, conscience, divine revelation, human freedom, etc." [9] These First Amendment clauses, he insists,

answer none of the eternal human questions with regard to the nature of truth and freedom or the manner in which the spiritual order of man's life is to be organized or not organized. Therefore they are not invested with the sanctity that attaches to dogma, but only with the rationality that attaches to law. . . . In a word, they are not articles of faith but articles of peace, that is to say, you may not act against them, because they are law and good law.[10]

"Like the rest of the Constitution," he continues, "these provisions are the work of lawyers, not of theologians or even of political theorists." [11] As lawyers "they had a strong sense of that primary criterion of good law which is its necessity or utility for the preservation of the public peace, under a given set of conditions." [12] Nor is this to be despised: "social peace, assured by equal justice in dealing with possibly conflicting groups, is the highest integrating element of the common good." [13] Anything other than religious liberty would, at the time of our national origin, have been catastrophic in view of the large number of unchurched, the multiplicity of denominations, the problems of economic trade, and the background of widening religious freedom in England.[14] Subsequent American experience has, moreover, abundantly confirmed the wisdom of the religion clauses of the First Amendment as practical policy. Concluding, Fr. Murray remarks that the American Catholic should refuse "to make an ideological idol out of religious freedom and separation of church and state" and that "he takes the highest ground available in this matter of the relations between religion and government when he asserts that his commitment to the religion clauses of the Constitution is a moral commitment to them as articles of peace in a pluralist society." [15]

Father Murray's position has all the more appeal because it is not logically derived from his Catholicism as such. It could as easily have been outlined by an equally reflective Protestant, Jew, or Moslem. It could form the basis of a broad social consensus on the value of religious liberty in a way that doctrine dependent upon particular religious presuppositions could not. Moreover, it is an appeal that is solidly rooted in historical fact, for no historical fact is more abundantly clear than that religious persecution does not contribute to social peace or harmony among religious groups. In the absence of adequate doctrinal support for religious liberty, there is thus every evidence that it would, in fact, still be good political policy.

But the fact that the "article of peace" approach does not derive from religious faith as such also constitutes its weakness. A solution designed simply to preserve peace and harmony will, for the Christian, remain open to the possibility of negation by more ultimate norms. Let us assume, for instance, that the issue of religious liberty could thus be resolved disregarding altogether faith in God. But suppose one's faith in God were to intrude and upset the solution. The Christian would be confronted with the question whether or not to continue to hold his faith in God; that is, whether to continue to be a Christian.

Christians in many eras have preferred violence and bloodshed to acquiescing to the presence of alien beliefs, and they have considered peace in such circumstances the most servile disobedience of God. They have ample precedent in Samuel, who bitterly condemned King Saul for being insufficiently destructive in the war of vengeance against the Amalekites (I Sam. 15). Anticipating this kind of objection, Fr. Murray has based a large part of his discussion of religious liberty on the fact that there has been a great deal of historical development in human sensitivity since those times. One could say that time, not abstract logic, has made such ancient good uncouth; that a more pragmatic basis of religious liberty does not risk relapse to the crude conceptions of social good which burdened the past precisely because experience has taught its lessons well.

I am not sure. There is too much religious repression occurring in the world at this very moment. And relapse from pragmatic tolerance to principled intolerance has occurred within individuals and groups often enough in the past (may one cite Augustine?) to suggest there must be a better way.

Murray's position, valuable as its contribution doubtless is, may also raise the old problem of thesis-hypothesis, the traditionalist Roman Catholic position which we have already discussed and which he opposes. Since he has expressly argued for religious liberty on the basis of *American* conditions and *American* experience, he has left the door open for the denial of religious liberty in other contexts and possibly even in this context at a different time. "The American Catholic," he writes,

is entirely prepared to accept our constitutional concept of freedom of religion and the policy of no establishment as the first of our prejudices. He is also prepared to admit that other prejudices may obtain elsewhere—in England, in

Sweden, in Spain. Their validity in their own context and against the background of the history that generated them does not disturb him in his conviction that his own prejudice . . . has its own validity.[16]

His more recent and more general thought, which sees the exigencies of religious liberty in relation to the total movement of human history, is subject to the same observation. If the basis of religious liberty is to be found in the changed personal and political consciousness of contemporary man, how is one to do justice on the one hand to the injury and injustice suffered by many minorities in previous human history and, on the other hand, to the possibility of a future situation in which the personal and religious consciousness of a majority might support the persecution of a minority? [17]

Arguing from pluralism raises the question of *degrees* of pluralism. That is, it forces one to ask how much diversity or how radical the pluralism should be to make religious liberty a rational, prudent social policy. For example, assuming the isolation of Spain from the effects of other cultural forces from outside, would the thirty thousand Protestants in that country of thirty million be enough to constitute "religious pluralism"? Undoubtedly the thirty thousand Protestants would feel that there were enough of them to justify their religious liberty; but would the majority concur? In the days of American "Protestant pluralism," the miniscule Roman Catholic minority often suffered in situations where the various Protestant denominations were inclined to be more tolerant of one another. Those, therefore, who base religious liberty upon pluralism alone (in fairness it must be said that Murray employs other arguments as well) have an obligation to indicate where, and on the basis of what criteria, they draw the line between situations which are pluralistic and situations which are not. Wherever the line is drawn, if a line *is* drawn, the foundations of a genuinely principled religious liberty will have been threatened. It will have been implied that there is no *universal* demand for religious liberty implicit in the Christian faith when that faith is properly understood and relevantly applied in every time and place. While the argument from pluralism is calculated to find acceptance among all rational persons regardless of their religious viewpoint, non-Christians might be more reassured in the presence of Christian cultural successes to hear Christians base their support for religious liberty on Christian theological grounds.

One of the things that has rightly disturbed many non-Communists about the possibility of Communist success is the fact that it may be irrevocable since Communism has so generally seemed to follow the thesis-hypothesis approach. Most Americans, for instance, are suspicious when the claim is made by American Communists that the *American* Communist Party is in full accord with the American traditions of freedom of expression, for it can be observed all too easily that Communists have not hesitated to deny freedom of expression in countries where they have gained sufficient power to do so. A principled Marxist statement supporting freedom of expression in all its forms, backed up by Communist practice in Communist countries, could, as I have already suggested, do much to alleviate the fears of democrats all over the world.[18]

Finally, if pluralism is taken in its *most* radical sense (that is, in the sense that considers even the most homogeneous community—Vatican City or a Tibetan monastery—to be pluralistic because of the uniqueness of each person's religious experience), then many of the applications of the argument from pluralism either collapse or point toward a religious perspective which must be surveyed further. Later I shall argue that the universality of such a pluralism is indeed implicit in the Christian faith and that this fact is indeed highly relevant to the present inquiry. But this kind of radical pluralism is not to be understood as a recent historical development nor as the characteristic of only a few societies such as the American, but rather as a description of the human situation before God in every place and time.

3. Spiritual Dignity and Spiritual Freedom

When Christians have sought to base religious liberty explicitly on Christian doctrine, it is not surprising that they have so often related it to their understanding of spiritual dignity and spiritual freedom. It may well be argued that freedom is essential to Christian teaching about the nature of man and about man's response to God. Far from providing a sanction for coercion of religion, it can be shown that Christian faith is meaningless if it is not entered into freely. Whether one speaks of Christian faith in terms of a trusting, loving disposition, as in the faithful relationship between God and man, or in the sense of the intellectual acceptance of truths which cannot be proved, it is apparent that freedom is absolutely fundamental. Love cannot be a command performance, or it loses its character as love. Conformity can be imposed, but genuine trust and belief obviously cannot. Attitude and belief are at the center of personal being, and both immediately lose their meaning to a person if they are imposed upon him.

These observations, which most Christians would share, can be supported in various ways by reference to Christian scripture and theological reflection.

It can be argued that man, as he has been created in the image of God (Gen. 1:26-27), is endowed with dignity and freedom. Just as dignity and freedom are essential to the nature of God, they are basic to the nature of man. As Gregory of Nyssa put it, "it is man's freedom which constitutes his resemblance to God." Therefore, "to use violence to force man to accept the Gospel would have been contrary to human dignity." [19] When man is coerced he is dehumanized, robbed of his essential nature. This is not only an obvious tragedy for him, it is also a frustration of the scripturally declared intention of God in the creation of man. Thus the denial of religious freedom to any man may be understood theologically as an affront to God. Those, therefore, who coerce others in religious matters for the sake of God are wrong. Ironically they are the ones who have set themselves most decisively *against* God and have most abundantly earned divine displeasure. A policy of religious liberty can thus be founded upon the dignity of man as created by God. This line of approach obviously has much in common with nontheological arguments for freedom on the basis of the inviolability of the human conscience—the notion that when man's conscience is coerced man has himself been destroyed, thereby nullifying any moral objective sought through coercion.

Furthermore, one can emphasize that freedom from spiritual tyranny belongs at the very heart of Christian doctrines of grace and redemption. Following Paul, particularly in the letters to the Galatians and Romans, it can be emphasized that *eleutheria,* or that freedom which is the gift of the Holy Spirit, is at the center of the Christian faith: "For freedom Christ has set us free; stand fast therefore, and do not submit again to a yoke of slavery" (Gal. 5:1). "For the law of the Spirit of life in Christ Jesus has set me free from the law of sin and death" (Rom. 8:2). "For I am sure that neither death, nor life, nor angels, nor principalities, nor things present, nor things to come, nor powers, nor height, nor depth, nor anything else in all

creation, will be able to separate us from the love of God
in Christ Jesus our Lord" (Rom. 8:38-39). Essential to
Paul's thought is the notion that in his pre-Christian experience man has indeed been tyrannized; not only by
external authorities (on occasion) and the strivings of his
bodily passions (typically), but (paradoxically) even by
religious law and custom. Religious law is depicted by
Paul as a curse. This is because it demands a humanly impossible perfection. But it is also a curse because even if
it were possible for human beings to be perfect, their perfection would be that of slaves perfectly obeying their
masters. Spiritually they would not be alive. Indeed, on
the basis of Paul's thought, it could be argued that those
who seek salvation by means of obedience to religious law
are essentially driven by selfish motives. Those who rely
upon faith in the divine grace of God as revealed in Christ
are, instead, governed by love. No longer is their relationship with God on an external level. Now they can approach
him on terms so intimate as to justify their calling him
"papa" (Gal. 4:6). "So through God you are no longer
a slave but a son, and if a son then an heir" (Gal. 4:7). In
such sonship it is understood that those things which
previously have exercised tyranny over man, summarized
as "sin and death," have been overcome. Moreover, and
this is crucial to our theme, it is recognized that this salvation, this freedom, is conferred by faith in God as revealed
in Christ. There is no apparent way in which salvation,
thus conceived, could be reduced to a matter of political
or even ecclesiastical policy. Neither state nor church can
make people "be religious." The moment they try they
merely confirm those forms of bondage which have characterized man's pre-Christian state of being. In other
words, any law of church or state designed to make people
be Christian would, if obeyed, more precisely succeed in

making them *not* be Christian. Christians, therefore, logically refrain from coercing the conscience of others themselves. And for the sake of their understanding of God's ways with men they resist every such effort by others.

But is this a matter of *inner* freedom, of a sort unaffected by outward conditions? In a certain sense, of course, Paul does affirm an inner freedom which remains free despite outward tyranny (as in the above quotation from Romans 8). Christians following Paul believe that salvation and spiritual freedom *can* occur under even the most totalitarian circumstances, a proposition which has undergone successful test on numerous occasions through the centuries.

But life is social. Salvation pertains to a quality of relationship with God, and it issues in a kind of relationship with other persons. The full richness of Christian life must be actualized in the context of society, in words and deeds bearing witness to the relationship with God. Unless man is externally free to bear witness to God, the inner intention of the covenant between God and man remains frustrated. This is to say again that God himself is impeded in his intentions. While God has indeed been able to work through responsive men in even the most adverse circumstances, such circumstances are to be understood as impedimenta to be removed by Christians who seek to "make straight in the desert a highway for God" (Isa. 40:3). Religious coercion must be understood as such an impedimentum.

Some Christian thinkers, such as Franklin H. Littell, arrive at similar conclusions through a doctrine of the church. "Voluntaryism and religious liberty," writes Littell,

rest upon the profound understanding that *that religious service only is pleasing to God which is voluntary and un-*

coerced. In pre-biblical religions, the gods were used by men to hold society together, to bless political systems and even military conquest. In the Bible, however, God requires obedience and service to *His* purpose—and He even creates a people whose very existence is based on that function.[20]

Since obedience to God must be voluntary and free, the appropriate form of church government is the free church. In addition to excluding the established church on the face of it, this conception similarly would exclude religious coercion as being alien to God's intention. Indeed, religious coercion can thus be identified as resulting from and in idolatry—worshiping as God what is in fact less than God. Discipline within the free church can and should be strict, but it reflects the voluntary fruits of the spirit.[21]

Another theological approach, similar to the foregoing, is that of the Danish theologian Niels H. Søe, who relates spiritual freedom to a doctrine of the cross. The cross is central in the Christian message as a symbol of the humility with which God has disclosed his love for men. Such love is utterly alien to any display of power or attempts to coerce the human will. The basis of religious liberty, writes Søe,

is the very fact that Christ did not come in heavenly splendour and worldly majesty to subjugate any possible resistance and force all and everybody to subjection. Christ made himself of no reputation and took upon him the form of a servant and humbled himself even unto the death of the cross. . . . Never did he do anything to force people into obedience and submission. Finally he was crucified through weakness, as Paul has it.[22]

The spectacle of the burning of a heretic at the stake for the sake of the gospel becomes grotesque when placed in the perspective of the cross, and in that perspective every denial of religious liberty in principle seems based upon a tragic misunderstanding of the nature of the Christian faith.

Some may object to the applicability of the foregoing theological justifications for religious liberty on the ground that some scripture and subsequent theological tradition has advanced a theological determinism: the notion that some are predestined to be saved by divine grace for the life of freedom of the spirit while others are predestined to spiritual death and hell. This tradition, based upon certain passages in Paul and identified particularly with Augustine and Calvin, would indeed appear to undercut religious liberty by questioning its psychological basis. Why need there be a social policy of religious liberty if man is not even free within himself? In response to this, it must be said that while theological determinism raises serious philosophical issues relating to the freedom of the will, it is itself based not on the philosophical problem but on an analysis of the source of spiritual power. Grace, paradoxically, is the source of *freedom* from the bondage of sin and death even in theological conceptions which consider some preordained to such freedom while others are predestined to a life of sin and death. Freedom, thus, remains an important psychological reality even in so unlikely a doctrine as the theological determinism which has been advanced by some Christian thinkers.

Approaching religious liberty through the doctrines of spiritual dignity and spiritual freedom, then, has clear advantages and few obvious disadvantages. Such doctrine is obviously Christian and apparently relevant. It has, moreover, commended itself to Christian thinkers of many generations and wide-ranging denominational viewpoints. It is the approach generally employed by those (principally

European) contemporary Roman Catholics who seek to ground religious liberty theologically. More recently it has, as we have seen, supplied the principal grounding for the theological portion of the Declaration on Religious Liberty by the Second Vatican Council, suggesting incidentally that the position lends itself as good common ground for further dialogue on issues of religious liberty between Protestants, Roman Catholics, and others. Why is it necessary to classify this approach as an "inadequate foundation"?

It must be said immediately that, notwithstanding difficulties in the position as a *sufficient* theological basis, it is a *necessary* part of any full statement of the Christian position. But I do not believe it is adequate.

As a preliminary thought, it is worth remembering that "spiritual freedom" and the uncoercibility of man's response to God have been affirmed eloquently by many Christian leaders and theologians who have also found it possible to advocate policies of repression. One recalls here again Cromwell's statement that, while he would "meddle with no man's conscience," this could not extend to noninterference with the objective act of the celebration of Mass. St. Augustine, the Reformers, and even St. Thomas Aquinas would all have agreed fully with the importance of spiritual freedom and with the necessity of man's being free to obey God and witness to God in the social context. But to a greater or lesser degree these thinkers also advocated the repression of heretics. It is not enough to say that such thinkers merely compartmentalized their theological reflection apart from practical policy, with the full implications of the one not permitted to define the other. The truth is that social or political freedom is not a direct corollary to that freedom which the Christian finds in Christ or to the general principle of the uncoercibility of the conscience. With few exceptions, Christian thinkers have also understood that life in society must be governed by law and that men must be restrained from injuring one another. Freedom from coercion might be possible, indeed, if all were Christian. But since not all are, there must be law and regulation. As Luther expressed the matter classically,

Certainly it is true that Christians, so far as they themselves are concerned, are subject neither to law nor sword, and have need of neither. But take heed and first fill the world with real Christians before you attempt to rule it in a Christian and evangelical manner. This you will never accomplish; for the world and the masses are and always will be un-Christian, even if they are all baptized and Christian in name.[23]

In the same writing, he warned against wicked people who might "under the name of Christian abuse evangelical freedom, carry on their rascality, and insist that they were Christians subject neither to law nor sword, as some are already raving and ranting." If freedom to express one's religious convictions in the social context were made into an absolute, there is no limit to the chaos which might result.

Similarly the argument that since God does not coerce the conscience neither should man is a weak argument. As Dean Kelley has remarked, "God himself does not use force to prevent murder or other heinous crimes which men seek to prevent or punish on their own initiative; so on the same ground some have claimed a mandate to combat heresy by violent means." [24] The reason is that thinkers like Augustine, the Reformers, and Thomas Aquinas have all believed that the open proclamation of heretical doctrine can have injurious effects upon the immortal souls of *other* people and upon the social context generally. For the protection of others, for the well-being of society, the freedom of some must sometimes be limited.

One can say, as a matter of fact, that if the expression of religious conviction (witness) has *effect,* then the expression of misleading errors will have *bad* effect. The very arguments which bridge between the freedom of the spirit and the necessity of its social expression boomerang to force consideration of what kinds of expressions are good for society and what kinds are bad, because the social effects of both kinds of expression are taken seriously. Making straight in the desert a highway for God, the removal of impediments to his purposes and intentions among men, can be interpreted as a matter of protecting God's weak ones from the corrupting influences of bad doctrine. Furthermore, while no one can directly control what anyone thinks, the social expression of bad doctrine to a certain degree can be prevented or controlled.

The weakness of the spiritual freedom argument as basis for religious liberty is one of the reasons why Fr. Murray sought a juridical basis instead for the Declaration on Religious Liberty of the Vatican Council. Reflecting upon his disagreement over this matter with French theologians, a disagreement which helped account for the delay in passage of the document, he remarked that "it is not obvious that the inference from freedom of conscience to the free exercise of religion as a human right is valid." [25] One can easily agree with this view of Fr. Murray, although the alternatives he proposes have problems of their own.

4. The Ethical Argument

In light of the difficulties which seem to attach to juridical and theological bases for religious liberty, it is not surprising that various Christian thinkers have foresworn such attempts to base policy upon principle and have sought rather to base it upon love. Even thinkers who see validity in other arguments are likely also to consider religious liberty an ethical problem which must be approached in such terms.

The Christian understands that he is ethically bound to seek the good in every situation. Disagree with others as he may, he will still love them if he is a real Christian. Love involves treating other persons with deepest respect, seeking their highest welfare. To Christians who perceive this responsibility in the Kantian sense of respect for personality as an end in itself, the case for religious liberty would seem nearly self-evident. For all Christians, the savage repressions and even demonic cruelties of the Inquisition, of burnings at the stake and torturings to wring out some meaningless confession of faith, of witch trials and condemnations—all represent the most obvious bankruptcy of Christian love however intricately they may be rationalized as necessary to preserve the unity of the faith or to maintain "Christian" civilization. Love has a way of penetrating tortured logic with a deeper truth. It is like the response of the Christ figure to the intricately structured speech of Dostoevski's "Grand Inquisitor": no hostility, no reasoned rebuttal, no defensiveness—simply a kiss of compassion.

Since all Christians agree on the central importance of love, the ethical argument seems also the best meeting ground for all those who, in the name of Christ, seek to preserve religious liberty. Significantly, recent Roman Catholic writers have, on the basis of Christian love and application of the "Golden Rule," urged that non-Catholics be afforded religious liberty by Catholics where the latter have superior power. For example, the Jesuit writer Albert Hartmann suggests that love moves the Christian beyond mere "tolerance" in his relations with persons of other faiths to a more affirmative relationship.[26] One may discern here the lengthened shadow of St. Francis of Assisi, about whom the sultan is supposed to have remarked that if all Christians were like him there would be no cause for conflict between Christian and Moslem.

Such considerations largely move the argument of Thomas G. Sanders, who urges Protestants to view church-state problems primarily as ethical problems. After surveying five main Protestant concepts of church and state and noting their abrupt differences and the extreme improbability of early reconciliation among them, Sanders suggests that accommodation can occur in the realization that "the issues called church-state problems really are problems of social and political ethics." [27] "In the coming decades," he writes,

Protestants must bring such problems within an ethical context, rather than leaving their determination to nonreligious, nonethical norms. The responsibility of a church for society as a whole may not correspond to its own self-interest; compromise may be necessary between institutional concerns and the equally valid responsibility of the church for a just society in which the interests of all groups and of the total society gain partial satisfaction. It is reasonable that what is good for Protestantism is *not* necessarily good for all of society.[28]

Involved here is recognition not only of much confusion in Protestant theory, but also an appreciation for the uniqueness of situations. Christians, acting in love, must be free to approach different situations with creative freshness.

Solutions to church-state problems take place within the context of particular church-state structures. The issues faced by the East German or Swedish churches are not those of the American churches. To base one's strategy on approximating the American system of church-state independence in Sweden smacks of irrelevance. Responsible action deals with the problems in a given context. . . . Discussion of even so general an issue as religious liberty has been inhibited in larger ecumenical groups like the World Council of Churches because churches with different relations to the state have brought different conceptions to the forum.[29]

The ethical approach suggested here seems especially indebted to such thinkers as Karl Barth and the American theologian Paul Lehmann, whose book *Ethics in a Christian Context* has made much of the importance of creative love in unique situations, in contrast to fixed universal principles.

The relevance of such views to situations of ideological conflict and religious persecution cannot be denied. In his book *Communism and the Theologians,* Charles C. West has made striking use of this approach in discussing the conflict between Marxism and Christianity. Marxism, he observes, bases its repudiation of religion largely upon the supposition that religion merely reflects the self-interest (the "ideological taint") which so-called "religious" persons have acquired in a given social structure. It provides a halo of justification of that interest. An adequate Christian response must, of course, make clear that the Christian faith is not thus bound to class interest—indeed, that it must often be prophetically critical of it. But West goes on to point out that the Christian, with his own understanding of the nonideological nature of man, is in a position to reverse the question and show that the ideological character of Marxism itself reduces and distorts man's humanity. Man, to the Christian, is more than anything that can be portrayed ideologically. Accordingly the best

clue to human relationships is not even to establish ideological common ground. Rather it is to move directly
across whatever ideological gaps do in fact exist and to relate to the other as a human being with authentic human
concerns. The Christian faith is relevant because it ad-
dresses such issues as posed by life and death or good and
evil, for these are the real human concerns. Although
ideological issues may have some provisional importance,
the real issues of life need to be faced creatively with love
in whatever life situation it has pleased God to place this
or that branch of the church and this or that Christian.
Applied to the question of religious liberty, the approach
would be to consider all political philosophies and legal
structures relative to the underlying drama of love seeking response, but it would also assume that love cannot
coerce response. Love has no motive to coerce, but only to
seek the good of the other.

While such a perspective may lack that ideological clarity which some seek, it moves the question of religious
liberty and church-state relations out of the courtyard and
into the main sanctuary of Christian faith where life is
really lived. As Sanders has put it, "failure to relate these
issues to ethics accounts for the strange sterility of church-
state actions in most denominations, reflected in their inclination to base positions on legal arguments, slogans,
anti-Catholicism, or self-interest." [30] The recovery of an
ethical approach might even reveal that many of the issues
which have seemed so crucial are not, Christianly speaking, of any importance at all.

But this approach, too, must be considered an "inadequate foundation." The problem is that Christian ethical
thought has typically understood that love by itself is not
the same thing as a social policy. Indeed it has generally
recognized that love may not unambiguously be translated

into social policy. The reason is partly that an attitude of good will, improperly instructed as to the *nature* of the good, may achieve not good but evil results. Paradoxically, actions which result in some evil may sometimes be necessary for the sake of the best possible good—in spite of protestations that ends do not justify means. A social policy based simply on love or ethics must come to grips with what Luther called the "strange" work of love; the love which must do negative things to achieve positive ends. Following Romans 13 and I Peter, Luther argued the necessity of the coercive restraint of evil by the state as an act of love for those who are thereby protected. As we have noted, Luther considered it mere sentimentality to try to govern the world as if everybody were already a Christian. While the Christian should not, in love, resist evildoers for his own sake, for the sake of protecting innocent third parties "he may and should seek vengeance, justice, protection, and help, and do as much as he can to achieve it. . . . In behalf of another . . . he may and should wield [the sword] and invoke it to restrain wickedness and to defend godliness." [31] The logic of this position is apparently affirmed wherever Christians support in principle the coercive power of the state.

While in the writing just quoted Luther specifically excluded coercive control of heresy ("Heresy can never be restrained by force"), numerous Christian thinkers have considered the suppression of heresy to be an act of love for those who might otherwise be contaminated. In later years even Luther came around to this position. Thomas Aquinas justified the Inquisition on similar grounds, arguing even that strict limits should be placed on the number of times a heretic should be permitted to recant:

Now if heretics who return were always taken back, so that they were kept in possession of life and other temporal goods, this might possibly be prejudicial to the salvation of others; for they would infect others, if they relapsed, and also if they escaped punishment others would feel more secure in lapsing into heresy. . . . Therefore, in the case of those who return for the first time, the Church not only receives them to Penance, but preserves their lives, and sometimes by dispensation restores them to their former ecclesiastical position, if they seem to be genuinely converted. . . . But when, after being taken back, they again relapse . . . they are admitted to Penance, if they return, but not so as to be delivered from sentence of death.[32]

Despite the mercy of the church, stubborn heretics must be excommunicated by her and given a death sentence by a secular court for the sake of "the safety of others." [33]

Augustine argued that love is not inconsistent with constraint and viewed the forcible disciplining of erring souls as beneficial not only to third persons who might become infected with the error but also to the heretic himself.[34] The Inquisition typically viewed heresy as a detestable and dangerous crime and provided the more sensitive of its functionaries with the scholastic reassurance that "persecution was a work of charity, for the benefit of the persecuted." [35] So long as one does in fact view error as subject to absolute human judgments from the Christian perspective, the logic of this position is not easily refuted on the grounds of "love." "The law," says Paul, "was our custodian until Christ came, that we might be justified by faith. But now that faith has come, we are no longer under a custodian" (Gal. 3:24-25). Cannot in Christian charity a case be made for similar guardianship against self-inflicted spiritual damage and the corrupting of society—just as one does not permit a toddling child to wander into the street or a teen-ager to steal automobiles?

In a helpful analysis of the negative means which Christians have sometimes felt compelled to employ, as during the Inquisition, John C. Bennett remarks that religious persecution must have been repellent to sensitive Christian spirits who, nevertheless, felt it to be necessary even for the sake of the persecuted.[36] For our purposes it is enough to observe that they felt the need for it and pursued it for what was a supposedly higher good. There is no way to calculate the tragedy and suffering which have resulted directly from the misguided efforts of well-intentioned Christians, and nowhere is this observation better founded than in the history of religious persecution.

Love, surely, must remain the attitude of Christians as they seek to approach any problem with understanding. With it, even mistaken or fuzzy notions may be spared many evil consequences. Without it, even the most correct principles may provide occasion for gross injustice. Yet, despite the centrality of love, good will alone is not enough. It is also necessary to understand the good and to pursue it rationally.

5. The Limited State

We must finally examine the view that there are limitations inherent in political power which preclude its proper involvement in matters of religion. This fifth basis for religious liberty has been developed in many ways, frequently in combination with one of the bases explored above. Indeed, however the principle of religious liberty is justified, it would seem to require an idea of the limited state as a consequence. But some writers have preferred to derive the principle from analysis of the state rather than from other grounds.

This has been done theologically, often through this or that exposition of the text "render to Caesar the things that are Caesar's, and to God the things that are God's"

77

(Luke 20:25). The medieval concept of the two swords was of this order. While the spiritual sword was considered by the religious authors of the doctrine to be superior to the temporal sword, they implied that each had a kind of independent existence. In the great medieval debates over church and state, both papacy and empire made claims amounting to their respective supremacy. It was never suggested that church and state were precisely balanced, but it was always assumed that the spiritual role of the state had *some* limitations, as did the temporal role of the church. Luther's doctrine of the two regiments or governments, the earthly and the spirtual, similarly denies the final authority of the state over religious matters and vice versa.

The related Lutheran doctrine of orders of creation is an intriguing theological approach to the assertion of the limited state. In recent years this approach has been developed most strikingly by Emil Brunner.[37] Reacting specifically against contract theories of society which reduce all forms of community to the relations of persons as individuals to one another through the state, Brunner insists that forms of community which are lower than the state have their own intrinsic nature and rights insofar as they reflect the orders of creation. Marriage and the family, labor and the economic order, religion and the church, politics and government are all ordained through the creation of God. The various orders of creation cannot simply be reduced to the state as if they were merely creatures of the state.[38] The state is defined by the monopoly of force which it legitimately holds in the interests of maintaining justice. Even here it properly employs coercion only as a substitute for voluntary justice. The state thus undertakes only what cannot be done by smaller units and what involves necessary use of coercive power.[39] When the state oversteps those bounds and interferes with other orders the result is the kind of catastrophe which Brunner finds amply illustrated in the modern totalitarian state. Such serious berakdowns in western society can only be repaired through recovery of the organic integrity of the orders in their mutually complementary wholeness.

The Roman Catholic principle of subsidiarity is similar. As stated classically by Pope Pius XI, it holds that

It is a fundamental principle of social philosophy, fixed and unchangeable, that one should not withdraw from individuals and commit to the community what they can accomplish by their own enterprise and industry. So, too, it is an injustice and at the same time a grave evil and a disturbance of right order, to transfer to the larger and higher collectivity functions which can be performed and provided for by lesser and subordinate bodies. Inasmuch as every social activity should, by its very nature, prove a help to members of the body social, it should never destroy or absorb them.[40]

The Roman Catholic application of the principle is not directly analogous to Brunner's "orders," but both clearly retain the highest respect for the integrity and relative independence of nonpolitical social forms within the organic wholeness of society. Both conceptions involve the notion that the most basic human rights and social forms are derived from God, not from the state. Ecumenical statements by the World Council of Churches have affirmed the same point. Typical of these is the statement of Section IV of the 1948 Amsterdam Assembly that "It is presumptuous for the state to assume that it can grant or deny fundamental rights. It is for the state to embody these rights in its own legal system and to ensure their observance in practice."

79

Similar things have also been said from nontheological orientations, particularly where absolutism or totalitarianism has been criticized. An unusually thorough analysis of the limited state has been provided by Professor Robert M. MacIver, who writes with great competence at the intersection of political science and sociology. In his work, *The Web of Government*,[41] MacIver has emphasized the distinction between the state and the community. Man's basically social nature finds expression in a rich fabric of associational forms in relation to which government is understood as the formal point of overall organization. No government could possibly comprehend, much less substantially control, the infinitely complex web of community life. "Every society," he writes, "at every stage of civilization, rests on a firmament of law that is vastly greater and much more intricate than any ever devised by any government, one that is too great and too intricate to be completely overturned even by the most revolutionary of governments." Even power is ubiquitous and complex in its organization. "The power wielded by government constitutes only one of several foci and kinds of power within a society—a consideration entirely ignored by the traditional myth of sovereignty." While political power "alone is the organ of the whole community," requiring and demanding the "obedience of all who live within its territory, without regard to faith or class or race," this does not mean that "all other social organizations are merely parts of the inclusive political organization." "This assumption of Hegelian and totalitarian dogma has never been in accord with social realities." When government tries to impose controls over the cultural life of society in the attempt to become all-embracing, it can succeed only in killing the creative spontaneity of culture, and reducing society to "a lifeless mechanism." [42]

In evaluating these lines of argument it is necessary to observe that not everybody who has argued the case of limited government has been committed to religious liberty as a universal principle. This would hold especially with regard to the Roman Catholic statements of subsidiarity, even though that principle could be interpreted as a basis for general religious liberty as distinct from liberty only for a one true church. The doctrine of orders, while employed in support of religious liberty by such writers as Emil Brunner, can be used with opposite effect to justify state actions in behalf of the religious order, as represented not by all religions but by the one which is understood to have been ordained by God. While Brunner would not draw this kind of conclusion, its logical possibility has been illustrated amply by others.

It is also necessary to make careful distinctions between theories of the actual limitation of the state and those of normative limitation. To the former, the state is seen as being limited *in fact*. To the latter, the state *ought* to be limited. Language employed by spokesmen for the limited state not infrequently confuses this necessary distinction, as in the World Council of Churches statement quoted above that "it is presumptuous for the state to assume that it can grant or deny fundamental rights." By speaking of God as the source of human rights, the World Council obviously intended to make a normative statement, that is, that the state *ought* to recognize certain rights because they are implicit in God's intentions for man. Surely the Council would not have asserted the state's lack of power to do just about anything it pleases respecting rights, for states have illustrated their ability to run roughshod over human rights from time immemorial. In a helpful analysis of the problem of rights, which will be considered in greater detail in chapter V, Professor Sidney Hook has reminded us that all rights, though established and maintained by political power, reflect an ethical understanding of the relationship which men ought to have with one another and with society as a whole.[43] But for present purposes it must be observed that when one advances beyond analysis of the state to *why* this or that "right" *ought* to be institutionalized and guaranteed by the state, one has moved again into question of bases for the rights other than the limitation of the state as such. From this perspective, in other words, the limitations-of-the-state argument has also proved to be an "inadequate foundation" for religious liberty.

Professor MacIver's analysis raises different questions because it asserts a factual consequence of denial of such rights as religious liberty, namely, that it would result in the destruction of what makes society vital and real. This argument can be taken more seriously, and it has a close interior relationship with the point of view which will be advanced in subsequent chapters. Two objections may be raised here, however, to its sole use as a basis for religious liberty. The first is theoretical, the second empirical. The theoretical problem is that it may beg the question concerning the normative society. I think I agree very substantially with MacIver's view according to which that society is best in which men are most creative and culture is spontaneously generated. But radically different views have certainly been advanced often enough by others. The idea of a "lifeless mechanism" might, indeed, correspond more adequately to the normative model implicit in much social thought, even as advanced by some theologians. This is particularly possible if a given set of cultural forms is considered to have been created by God himself and is thereby invested with sacredness and immutability. Even the Lutheran concept of orders has risked this interpretation insofar as it has tended to identify particular cultural forms with orders of creation which have been ordained by God. (Of course this is not necessarily implied by a doctrine of orders.)

The other objection to the simple use of an analysis such as that of MacIver as sole basis for religious liberty is that it may not take seriously enough the ability of the state to exercise positive control over the direction of society. If I understand MacIver correctly, the point is one of emphasis rather than of difference in principle. MacIver is clearly right in asserting that the state is not to be identified with society, and he is right likewise in pointing out that it is not simply one group alongside other groups. It is the apex of social organization, the point of formal integration of power and law. This is to say, I think, that the state is a *function* of society; that it is society acting as a whole, with the ability to compel.[44] The rapid increase in knowledge about society, coupled in many cases with a more profound ethical sensitivity as to the nature of justice, has increased the ability of society, acting as a whole, to improve the conditions of its own life. For good or ill, the state is present potentially in every aspect of life (be it ever so private or ever so religious) insofar as it is capable of controlling behavior. Even "thought control" is not an entirely meaningless expression, although the compatibility between ventures of this kind and the health of any society is rightly suspect.

It should perhaps be added to the foregoing that MacIver's warnings may not apply sufficient support for religious liberty in those societies which are virtually homogeneous in religious composition in their treatment of small minorities. In a quite homogeneous culture, it might not be too damaging empirically for small minorities to be coerced. Such coercion could be entirely unnoticed by most people. A kind of sociological basis for thesis-hypothesis could be thus outlined! But in any event, since the Christian does not worship society nor the vitality of society much as he may properly regard vital community life to be God's good intention for man, he must still seek his basic foundation for a doctrine of religious liberty in deeper theological reflection.

In summary it must be said that, although the various possible foundations for religious liberty discussed in this chapter have been considered "inadequate," all point in that direction and contribute to our understanding of the problem. I believe that a deeper basis is available, and the foregoing points, uncertain though they may be, sufficiently convince me that religious liberty is wise policy and that it should be supported by Christians and all other responsible persons.

The main problem with most of these "inadequate foundations" is that they may be undermined when they are held in common with an absolute conception of the truth or with an absolute idea of necessary means of salvation. Doctrines of spiritual freedom, love, limited state, and pluralism doubtless can condition the severity of any religious repression. But combined with absolute claims each could yield to this or that form of repression for the sake of truth, or God's intention for man, or even as a work of love, however strange. I believe it can be argued truthfully that absolute claims are incompatible with a thoroughgoing principle of religious liberty, although the element of ambiguity or at least of paradox in such a statement must be admitted and scrupulously examined. In the next two chapters we shall examine the question whether Protestant faith, basically understood, provides a way to avoid absolute claims without at the same time destroying itself.

NOTES

[1] *We Hold These Truths: Catholic Reflections on the American Proposition* (New York: Sheed and Ward, 1960).

[2] The significance of this Manifesto as a Protestant commitment to American national traditions is underscored by the fact that it was signed by such highly influential Protestant leaders as Methodist Bishop G. Bromley Oxnam, *The Christian Century* editor Charles Clayton Morrison, President John A. Mackay of Princeton Theological Seminary, President Edwin McNeill Poteat of Colgate-Rochester Divinity School, Dr. Louie D. Newton, president of the Southern Baptist Convention, and Dr. Joseph M. Dawson, executive secretary of the Baptist Joint Committee on Public Affairs.

[3] Cf. *From State Church to Pluralism: A Protestant Interpretation of Religion in American History* (Garden City, N.Y.: Doubleday, 1962).

[4] Cf. Sanders, *Protestant Concepts of Church and State,* pp. 218-20.

[5] *General Findings* of the National Study Conference on Church and State.

[6] Cf. Philip Wogaman, "The Changing Role of Government and the Myth of Separation," *A Journal of Church and State* (May, 1963).

[7] "The American Tradition of Religious Freedom: An Historical Analysis," *Journal of Public Law,* XIII, No. 2 (1964), 250 ff.

[8] *Protestant-Catholic-Jew: An Essay in American Religious Sociology* (Garden City, N.Y.: Doubleday, 1960), p. 85.

[9] *We Hold These Truths,* p. 48.

[10] *Ibid.,* p. 49.

[11] *Ibid.,* p. 56.

[12] *Ibid.,* p. 57.

[13] *Ibid.,* p. 58.

[14] *Ibid.,* pp. 58-59.

[15] *Ibid.,* p. 78.

[16] *Ibid.,* p. 47.

[17] This problem is especially raised by his recent essay *The Problem of Religious Freedom.* In an insightful critique of this work, A. F. Carrillo de Albornoz especially takes issue with Murray's statement that "The historical institutions of establishment and intolerance are to be judged 'in situ.' They might well be judged *valid* 'in situ.' . . . These institutions might well have been useful to people, in the condition of the personal and political consciousness of the people at that time." Arguing that such statements undercut a principled religious liberty, Carrillo continues: "We cannot help asking ourselves whether Fr. Murray's intention was to justify historically the Roman Catholic Church. In this case it is our con-

viction that the worst justification is that of affirming that every situation (even that most contrary religious liberty) may be valid 'in situ.' For in this case, if the Catholic Church were to make this thesis her own, she would appear more than ever as the main obstacle for an ecumenical understanding in matters of religious freedom." Cf. Carrillo, "Religious Freedom: Intrinsic or Fortuitous," *The Christian Century,* LXXXII, No. 37 (Sept. 15, 1965), 1122-26.

[18] I use this illustration because it vividly suggests to persons of the Christian West the theoretical difficulties of a position, but in using it I must make clear that there is no implied or intended comparison of Roman Catholicism with Communism.

[19] Quoted by Carrillo, *Roman Catholicism and Religious Liberty,* p. 28. Walter G. Mueder has formulated this insight in the following way: "Since God does not coerce the will of man, but has given the gift of faith and obedience in a freed decision of man, no lesser authority may set up a more ultimate coercion over his conscience. This applies to both church and state and is the basis for the claim that religious liberty is the most basic of all human rights." *Foundations of the Responsible Society* (New York and Nashville: Abingdon Press, 1959), p. 118.

[20] "Christian Witness and Culture-Religion," in *Preparatory Papers for the National Study Conference on Church and State* (privately published by the National Council of the Churches of Christ in the U.S.A., 1964), p. 6.

[21] Cf. Sanders, *Protestant Concepts of Church and State,* pp. 218 ff.

[22] Niels H. Søe, "The Theological Basis of Religious Liberty," in *The Ecumenical Review,* XI, No. 1 (1958), 40.

[23] "Temporal Authority: To What Extent It Should Be Obeyed," in *Luther's Works,* XLV (Philadelphia: Muhlenberg Press, 1962), 91.

[24] From a review of Carrillo's book, *The Basis of Religious Liberty* in *A Journal of Church and State,* VI, No. 3 (1964), 367.

[25] "This Matter of Religious Freedom," *America,* CXIII (Jan. 9, 1965).

[26] Quoted by Carrillo in *Roman Catholicism and Religious Liberty,* p. 31.

[27] Sanders, *Protestant Concepts of Church and State,* p. 292.

[28] *Ibid.,* p. 293.

[29] *Ibid.,* p. 294.

[30] *Ibid.,* p. 292.

[31] "Temporal Authority," *Luther's Works,* XLV, 101, 103.

[32] *Summa Theologica,* ii. Q. xi. Art. IV.

[33] *Ibid.,* Art. III.

[34] Professor Ronald H. Bainton has provided an interesting ex-

position of this aspect of Augustine's thought in the introduction to his edition of Sebastian Castellio's *Concerning Heretics* (New York: Columbia University Press, 1935), pp. 24-25.

[35] Henry Charles Lea, *A History of the Inquisition of the Middle Ages* (New York: The Macmillan Co., 1908), I, 241.

[36] *Christianity and Communism Today* (New York: Association Press, 1960), pp. 86-87.

[37] Cf. esp. *Justice and the Social Order* (New York: Harper and Brothers, 1945).

[38] *Ibid.,* pp. 65 ff.

[39] *Ibid.,* pp. 137-39.

[40] *Quadragesimo Anno.*

[41] Robert M. MacIver, *The Web of Government* (New York: The Macmillan Co., 1947).

[42] *Ibid.,* pp. 65, 87, 94, 445, 423.

[43] *The Paradoxes of Freedom* (Berkeley and Los Angeles: University of California Press, 1962), esp. pp. 4-13.

[44] It may be necessary to emphasize here, with Professor MacIver, that every state exists more or less by degrees of consent of the governed. No state could long exist as such if it were totally alienated from its people.

III

Protestant Faith as Criticism

It is humbling for Christians to realize that a number of able students of the problem of religious liberty consider the Hebrew-Christian tradition responsible, not for the articulation and defense of religious liberty, but for its denial. The basis of this indictment is evident and easily supported. It lies not simply on the factual history of religious persecution by persons of this tradition, but on analysis of the meaning of the primary Hebrew-Christian belief in the one God, Yahweh.

1. Monotheism and Intolerance

The universal monotheism of the Hebrew-Christian tradition seems automatically to define those who do not accept or worship God as being in error (at best) or possibly even as being the enemies of God. If the God I worship is the one true God, then obviously those who worship other gods are in error. Francesco Ruffini expressed this indictment more than half a century ago in these words:

When the idea of a single and universal God was set, first by the Hebrews and then by the Christians, against the ancient polytheism, there arose a new form of religious exclusivism, contrary to the old not less in its basis than in its effects. The gods of the other peoples were said to be false and fallen, and religion lost its national and public character, and became on the one side cosmopolitan and on the other proper to each individual. From this followed not only an inextinguishable spirit of proselytism, but also the principle that he only could be saved who worshipped the true God; that is to say, the principle of absolute intolerance.[1]

Leo Pfeffer has restated the thesis more recently in the following way:

It is substantially true that the problem of compulsion in religion is a heritage of the monotheistic worship which Moses commanded must, under penalty of death, be accorded to a jealous God. The history of religious persecution flows directly from Moses' command to slay the three thousand men who worshipped the golden calf to the Spanish Inquisition and the exiling of Roger Williams and Anne Hutchinson by the Puritan fathers.[2]

The reader may rightly question whether the Hebrew-Christian tradition (with its cousin, Islam) may properly be blamed for all religious persecution, even in the Western world. One can point to such persecution in the history of Greek culture as well. For example, note the principal charge lodged against Socrates by irate citizens who rightly saw the subversive implications of his questing spirit respecting their religious traditions. This was, of course, prior to the full flowering of Greek philosophy and might be considered the "birth pangs" of the new, more enlightened era which began with Socrates. But even later the Syrian Emperor Antiochus IV was to become so imbued with the spirit of Hellenistic enlightenment that he mercilessly persecuted the Jews of the second century B.C. after he rightly perceived them as a major obstruction to his design to spread that spirit more completely in his empire. These illustrations suggest that nonuniversal religions may also tend to universalize themselves, especially within a given community, and that universal claims of all kinds (including those based in the high culture of the Greeks) may have the same effect on freedom as the universal monotheism of the Hebrew-Christian tradition.

But this does not refute the charge that monotheism does have a negative effect on religious liberty. Despite the various exceptions which anybody could cite, it remains that the comparatively easygoing, tolerant spirit of paganism has lacked the same ground for persecution which is embedded in the monotheistic idea.

It is not surprising, therefore, that one may readily locate support for the frankest forms of intolerance in the Old Testament. In the book of Deuteronomy, for instance (where one may find deep ethical concern for justice expressed in compassionate laws), the following counsel of intolerance appears:

If your brother, the son of your mother, or your son, or your daughter, or the wife of your bosom, or your friend who is as your own soul, entices you secretly, saying, "Let us go and serve other gods," which neither you nor your fathers have known, some of the gods of the peoples that are round about you, whether near you or far off from you, from the one end of the earth to the other, you shall not yield to him or listen to him, nor shall your eye pity him, nor shall you spare him, nor shall you conceal him; but you shall kill him; your hand shall be first against him to put him to death, and afterwards the hand of all the people. (Deut. 13:6-9.)

There is striking precedent here for the setting of children against parents and friend against friend in modern totalitarian states! Or one may consider Leviticus, the book in which the famous love commandment appears ("you shall love your neighbor as yourself"). So also does the commandment that "he who blasphemes the name of the Lord shall be put to death; all the congregation shall stone him; the sojourner as well as the native, when he blasphemes the Name, shall be put to death" (Lev. 24:16). Nor can it be said that these statements merely represent an early, more primitive stage in the development of Hebrew religion. Deuteronomy probably reflects the late seventh century B.C., a full century after the great eighth-century prophets Amos, Hosea, Isaiah, and Micah. The book obviously is to some degree dependent upon the advanced ideas and sensitivities of these prophets. Leviticus evidently belongs to the period after the great Exile and is at least a century later.

Biblical history, indeed, reveals a fascinating paradox which helps to underscore how far intolerance could be carried on the basis of the covenant monotheism of the Hebrews. This paradox lies in the astonishing correlation of ideas concerning universal monotheism and Israel as a chosen people. The paradox is most clearly evident during the "priestly period" following the Exile when the loftiest statements of the universality of God appear in combination with the narrowest interpretations of the covenant community as the "chosen people." How, indeed, could the movement which produced the magnificent theological insights of the first chapter of Genesis or the

91

eighth Psalm, two statements of God's universal creative-
ness and rulership, also have produced Ezra's abject prayer
of confession for the "sin" of intermarriage between Hebrews and persons unable to trace their lineage from
Abraham and the consequent inhumanity of those who
set about to repair this damage (Ezra 9–10)? Whatever
answer one may choose to give, it is clear that the more
universal the claim concerning God, the greater was its
negative effect upon those who, for whatever reason, were
counted outside the covenant community. In this light,
the logic of the Hebrew faith would seem to compel a
high degree of religious intolerance and to permit the
repressive practices envisaged by Deuteronomy and Leviticus. As a matter of fact, the subsequent development of
monotheism in Judaism, Christianity, and Islam has in
nearly every age been accompanied by greater or lesser
degrees of intolerance and persecution (although Judaism
has more often been the victim than the perpetrator of
persecution for the past two millennia).

In the specifically Christian New Testament scriptures,
it is not so easy to document the correlation between
monotheism and intolerance, although some illustrations
can be found. It needs to be remembered, in comparing
the Old Testament with the New, that most of the Old
Testament scriptures were written during periods when
the Hebrews had considerable control over the civil regu-
lations of their own community. By contrast, Christians
were sectarian religiously and marginal politically during the much briefer time span in which the New Testament documents were written. During this period it would
not have occurred to a Christian leader to contemplate a
political policy toward non-Christians in a Christian state.
But an *attitude* of intolerance toward non-Christians (or
toward heretical Christians) is well illustrated by such

passages as II John 9-11 and II Peter 2:1. In the first of these, the writer asserts that

any one who goes ahead and does not abide in the doctrine of Christ does not have God; he who abides in the doctrine of Christ has both the Father and the Son. If any one comes to you and does not bring this doctrine, do not receive him into the house or give him any greeting; for he who greets him shares his wicked work.

In the second passage the writer says that "false prophets also arose among the people, just as there will be false teachers among you, who will secretly bring in destructive heresies, even denying the Master who bought them, bringing upon themselves swift destruction." Concerning such persons he adds that "these, like irrational animals, creatures of instinct, born to be caught and killed, reviling in matters of which they are ignorant, will be destroyed in the same destruction with them, suffering wrong for their wrongdoing." (2:12-13b.) These and similar teachings in the New Testament might readily be employed as bases for repressive civil policy in a state dominated by Christians. These quotations, of course, belong to the period when the New Testament church was rent by considerable internal struggle over doctrine. But even much earlier Paul placed himself on record with crisp distinctions between the fullness of Christian revelation and the folly of non-Christian world views. Thus, in I Corinthians he inquires "Where is the wise man? Where is the scribe? Where is the debater of this age? Has not God made foolish the wisdom of the world?" (1:20.) In II Corinthians, he cautions his Christian readers with these words which are apparently in opposition to intermarriage or even friendly contact between Christians and outsiders: "Do not be mismated with unbelievers. For what partnership have righteousness and iniquity? Or what fellowship has light with darkness? What accord has Christ with Belial? Or what has a believer in common with an unbeliever? What agreement has the temple of God with idols?" (6:14-16a.) In Colossians (presuming Pauline authorship), he urges Christians,

see to it that no one makes a prey of you by philosophy and empty deceit, according to human tradition, according to the elemental spirits of the universe, and not according to Christ. For *in him the whole fulness of deity dwells bodily,* and you have come to fulness of life in him, who is the head of all rule and authority. (2:8-10; italics mine.)

To repeat the question we have been pursuing: if there is but one God, and if he has manifested himself to a particular religious community, does this not automatically prejudice the truth claims of every other person who is outside that community? And does this not undermine the basis for religious liberty wherever the members of that community hold political power? At the very least one would have to admit that if this exhausts the logical applicability of monotheism, there is no hope that one might find in Christian faith a way to avoid the absolute claims which we have earlier asserted to be the root cause of religious intolerance.

2. Monotheism and Tolerance

At the same time, however, the idea of monotheism has another logical possibility which also is amply illustrated in biblical and postbiblical history. That is the notion that, since God transcends any man, culture, or society, it ill behooves any man to make pretentious claims on the basis of which intolerance and persecution might be grounded. If God is sovereign Lord of all, no man can justly claim to know all about God's intentions at every time and place in human history. No man can have unlimited confidence that God, the sovereign Lord of all the ages, has spoken only to him or to his community. Nor can any man have unlimited confidence in his own perceptions of the word which God *has* spoken to him. Latent beneath religious intolerance is the silent assumption of one's own absolute rightness. It is precisely this assumption which the second application of monotheism calls into question. If God is sovereign and transcendent, he is also to some extent hidden; and religious humility thus derives from recognition of the difference between Creator and creature.

This theme may never have been a very popular one, but it is richly present even in Old Testament history. For instance, several of the great prophets went so far in their criticism of the religious and nationalistic pretensions of their fellow Hebrews as to see God at work in the activities of even their most dangerous enemies. Isaiah thus pictures the dread Assyrian Empire as instrument of God's punishing wrath: "Ah, Assyria, the rod of my anger, the staff of my fury! Against a godless nation I send him, and against the people of my wrath I command him" (Isa. 10:5-6a). The "godless nation" here referred to is of course the Hebrew nation. A century later Jeremiah was to attribute the great successes of the Babylonians under Nebuchadnezzar to God ("I have given all these lands into the hand of Nebuchadnezzar, the king of Babylon, my servant. . .") and to urge Hebrew surrender to this new power (Jer. 27:6, 12). Later he wrote to the exiled Hebrews in Babylon to "seek the welfare of the city where I [the Lord] have sent you into exile, and pray to the Lord on its behalf, for in its welfare you will find your welfare" (Jer. 29:7). For this kind of advice Jeremiah was understandably ostracized by an irate citizenry, but his words were recorded. Still later, Deutero-Isaiah could speak of the Persian conqueror Cyrus—who probably would not have known the difference between the Hebrew God Yahweh and the Canaanite gods—as Yahweh's chosen servant: "Thus says the Lord to his anointed, to Cyrus. . ." (Isa. 45:1a). Cyrus, of course, did become the liberator of captive peoples, including the Hebrews, but his religious perspective certainly was not that of Deutero-Isaiah.

Even during the priestly period after the exile there is some evidence of a more tolerant "minority report"; witness the books of Ruth and Jonah, both of which likely belong to this period. Ruth, as protest against the ban on intermarriage, asserts that foreigners can come into the Hebrew covenant. This book even pictures the foreigner Ruth (from Moab) as having been the great-grandmother of King David himself. The book of Jonah depicts the compassion of God for the proverbially wicked Ninevites (Assyrians) and, with sly humor, contrasts the pig-headed religious chauvinism of the Hebrew Jonah with a broader understanding of God. Both of these writings, of course, speak of foreigners coming into the covenant community as converts. But both also stand as witnesses to a more liberal understanding of God during a time of great intolerance.

One can even generalize and say that all the great prophets, whose writings and utterances the Hebrews thought worthy of preservation, ventured to criticize the moral and religious pretensions of their fellows. Is not the reason for this the transcendence and sovereignty implicit in the Hebrew conception of God? He is not an instrument of Israel's purposes. His ways are not their ways. He takes no delight in their solemn assemblies. His day will not be for them a day of happiness and rejoicing but a gloomy day of judgment.

At the heart of the second application of monotheism is the rich Hebrew contrast between worship of the true God and idolatry. While this contrast receives a typically narrow interpretation at many points, such as in the previously quoted passages from Deuteronomy and Leviticus, it opens the door for more liberal treatment. Idolatry can be understood as the absolutizing of any limited perspective. The term, as richly interpreted in much contemporary Christian theology, may lie at the root of much religious intolerance. If this is so, then an important aspect of Christian support for religious liberty is latent in the second approach to monotheism. It is in the criticism of the element of idolatry in every absolute claim which might form the basis for religious persecution or repression.

But is this a possibility in the light of the specifically Christian Scriptures, the New Testament? I believe it is, despite the New Testament quotations which have already been presented. The Synoptic Gospels, which are the most dependable witness to the actual teachings of Jesus, generally portray the faithful disciple of Christ as one who is not pretentious in his religious life. Jesus' own most scathing criticism is directed, not at the "irreligious" sinners, publicans, and "peoples of the land," but at the most respectably religious people who thought themselves better than all others. The humble, the poor in spirit, the repentant alone are considered worthy of the Kingdom of God. They are to forgive others "seventy times seven." They are to love their enemies. They are not to judge others, leaving judgment to God alone. Nor is Jesus impressed by the supposed absolute sanctity of such religious institutions as the sabbath, and he does not hesitate to violate such institutions when necessary for a higher good. Here are all the elements of the critique of idolatry. Jesus is even happy to apply the second approach to monotheism with respect to himself: "Why do you call me good? No one is good but God alone." (Mark 10:18 and Luke 18:19; cf. Matt. 19:17.)

Can the second approach survive the Christologies of later New Testament writers, such as Paul and the writer of the Fourth Gospel? There is no reason why it should not, provided one does not venture arrogant claims regarding one's own complete understanding of the full meaning of Christ as the decisive revelation of God. One can in faith assert with Colossians that in Christ "the whole fullness of deity dwells bodily" without claiming thereby a full understanding of exactly what that assertion means. Indeed, the element of metaphor in such a statement must have been as apparent to the writer as it is to us, for he moves readily from passages asserting the unity of God in Christ to other passages where the distinction between God and Christ is clearly preserved.

One may rightly say that the Christian faith would lose its identity if it ceased to proclaim that in some sense Christ is authentically the revelation of the nature of God. But this does not require the Christian to claim finality in his understanding. To employ a human analogy, a five-year-old child may be able to identify his (human) father and to sense his essential qualities. But this does not mean that he understands his father as his father's adult friends do and as he himself will increasingly with maturation. Moreover, the decisive element of faith which is present in all human and religious relationships—so clearly grasped by Paul in his conception of justification—would seem more consonant with the second than with the first approach to monotheism. The commitment of faith may be decisive, and faith may be a necessary precondition for authentic revelations of ultimate reality. But faith, by definition, is not the same thing as certainty. It is interesting that, on the basis of God's gift of grace received through faith, Paul proclaimed the freedom of every man from slavish adherence to religious law and custom as if such adherence could bring one closer to God. In Galatians Paul is briskly critical of the idolatries of law and custom in which he himself had formerly found the center of life's meaning.

One must ask whether the second approach to monotheism would reduce the Christian position to skepticism. That question will be dealt with more completely in the following chapter, because it is a critically important one. For the moment, however, one may observe that there may be some real *value* to at least some degree of skepticism as a basis for religious liberty. Professor Mark De Wolfe Howe is typical of various commentators on religious liberty who have made this observation when he writes that

those who support the thesis that each man should be left free by government to follow the faith which his mind and heart prefer, very generally, if not invariably, have in religion abandoned the belief that an ultimate truth has been revealed for all and, as truth, is binding on all. The political conviction that religious liberty is of profound importance generally bespeaks a Protestant, and very frequently a skeptical, attitude towards the "truths" of religion.[3]

Postponing until later the problems posed by skepticism as such, it can nevertheless be said here that if uncertainty attaches to a system of religious belief or object of worship, a corresponding uncertainty clouds the value of coercing individuals or groups in the direction of such

99

belief or worship or of silencing alternative expressions of belief and worship. *If, at the heart of Christian understanding, there is criticism of every absolute certainty, no aspect of Christian teaching is of greater importance in the negative defense against denial of religious liberty.* Theological criticism of absolute claims has found significant expression in the work of three modern theologians, some of whose insights must now be related.

3. The Critical Realism of Reinhold Niebuhr

A consistent theme in most of the writings of Reinhold Niebuhr for more than a third of a century has been a deep realism regarding the fact of human sin and a sharp criticism of claims of perfection for human institutions past, present, or future. In the main, Niebuhr's judgments have been derived from his doctrine of man. He has portrayed man in terms of his sinful as well as good inclinations, and he has sought to expose man's tendencies to place himself at the heart of his world instead of acknowledging the rule of God. Man's pretensions are at the root of his most demonic accomplishments and explain his readiness to define his own interests in terms of universal good or truth. Such observations have more than passing relevance to the problem of religious liberty, particularly when they are applied to case histories of religious repression.

Niebuhr's essay on "Having, and Not Having, the Truth," in *The Nature and Destiny of Man* [4] has particular applicability as an instance of the Protestant critique of absolutes. Niebuhr does not deny the possibility of knowledge of the truth; this possibility, indeed, gains rich meaning through man's capacity for rational self-transcendence. But it is impossible "to accept *our* truth as *the* truth" because our "capacity for rational self-transcen-

dence opens up constantly new and higher points of vantage for judging our finite perspectives in the light of a
more inclusive truth." [5] Identification of *the* truth would
at least imply the cessation of this development. Moreover, "our involvement in natural and historical flux sets
final limits upon our quest for the truth and insures the
partial and particular character of even the highest cultural vantage point." Man's freedom suggests the unfold-
ing possibilities of truth, but his finitude limits his ability
to gain all the truth. The difficulties in identifying truth
are complicated by the fact that man tends to make "premature claims of finality" for what truth he does have,
thereby distorting the perspective in which it is held. They
are complicated further because in his sin man tends to
bend the truth to suit his own interests. He is at least more
inclined to see and emphasize those truths which are
most in accord with his own interests.

In response to the objection that, while man in his
fallen state is indeed limited in his understanding, redeemed man possesses final truth, Niebuhr observes that
the Reformation doctrine of Justification by Faith "pre-
supposed the imperfection of the redeemed." "Logically,"
he continues, "this includes the imperfection of 'redeemed'
knowledge and wisdom." Indeed, it was the failure by the
Reformation to be true to the full implications of its
principle of justification which resulted in the intolerance
which it so often practiced. Paradoxically, the "intolerant
fanaticism" of the Reformation

sprang from its failure to apply this insight to the cultural
problem so that it would mitigate the spiritual pride of man.
Its actions thus proved its theory to be correct; but they also
revealed it to be ineffective. It is a theory which must not
only be apprehended by the mind but which must enter

into the heart and break its pride. The authority of the Bible was used to break the proud authority of the church; whereupon the Bible became another instrument of human pride.[6]

Niebuhr proceeds, then, to criticize Roman Catholic claims (such as the direct identification of Christ with the "Sacred Host" on the altar) and to note the practical results of simple distinctions between truth and error in terms of intolerance (here he quotes from Catholic documents supporting the "thesis-hypothesis" approach which was much more dominant at the time of his writing). He proceeds also to criticize Protestant and Marxist intolerance, which is similarly based upon overlooking the limited character of human knowing. Concluding, he remarks that "no toleration is possible without a measure of provisional scepticism about the truth we hold," although we remain loyal to truth and affirm the possibilities of its attainment.

Here, then, is a theological analysis which frankly affirms a provisional skepticism as the surest foundation for tolerance and which is brutally critical of pretensions to absolute knowledge from whatever source.

I believe that Niebuhr's views retain their validity despite a sharp criticism from Niels H. Søe.[7] Professor Søe, who prefers to base religious liberty on the theological meaning of the Cross, criticizes Niebuhr's discussion on three basic grounds. In the first place, he finds in it only confirmation of certain Roman Catholic stereotypes of Protestantism as being based on modern relativism and skepticism, and he suggests its vulnerability therefore to Roman Catholic claims to preferred treatment on the ground of their sole possession of the truth. In the second place, he believes Niebuhr has overlooked the fact that there is no trace of relativism or skepticism in the New Testament: "As far as I can see both the Lord Himself and

His disciples are convinced that they are bearers of the untainted truth, the pure and unadulterated Gospel, God's own word." [8] And thirdly, he raises the question whether there can be a principled *theological* basis for tolerance without there being a commitment to the truth of Christian theology as over against other possibilities.

I do not believe these objections are decisive, although in responding to them one may help to clarify Niebuhr's position. The first objection seems particularly weak because, of course, the effect of Niebuhr's position is to expose the pretension of any claim to sole possession of truth, not to support it. There is greater power in recognition of limitations than in pretending that they do not exist. The fact that one recognizes limitations in the human situation does not weaken one's position vis-à-vis those who make absolute claims except in the sense that a fanatic may come out well in some forms of competition where narrowness of vision contributes to the concentration of energies. But for such purposes the various different kinds of absolutism seem interchangeable, irrespective of the question of truth. The second objection seems stronger, however, partly because Niebuhr has made little effort to proof-text his position. But there is, as we have suggested, abundant scriptural support for the kind of contentions upon which he bases his position. Indeed, along with the Reformation, his position represents an interpretation of the essence of the New Testament, and it finds considerable support in the writings of Paul and in the teachings of the Synoptic Gospels which bear upon the bases of humility. This points, however, to the third objection, which raises the whole question of the compatibility of any degree of skepticism with theological commitment to Christian faith as over against other alternative faiths and the logical issue whether skepticism is compatible with its own ultimate claims (how does one *know* that truth is limited, and is *that* truth limited, etc.?). Niebuhr, of course, is not a thoroughgoing skeptic, and in this work he clearly affirms a Christian commitment even while he insists that we recognize the limitations of the human knowledge situation. Moreover, he admits the possibility that we may know certainly that we are in fact finite creatures. These points are raised in anticipation of problems which will be discussed in the next chapter.

4. The "Radical Monotheism" of H. Richard Niebuhr

Similar criticism of human pretensions to have absolute truth is important in the thought of H. Richard Niebuhr, although the basis for his conclusions is strikingly different. Richard Niebuhr bases his analysis on the question of how men relate themselves to the centers of value which give meaning to their existence; that is to say, upon analysis of what men worship.[9] It is basic to his thought that all men do worship and that the question, therefore, is a universal one. All men have value centers on the basis of which they judge the value of other things. Value centers also form the basis of the "causes" to which men commit themselves and in loyalty to which they express their moral nature. While persons may be dispassionate or relatively objective about other things, they approach their value centers and pursue their causes with great intensity. Therefore, whenever a system of valuation or a loyalty is attacked (or persecuted) it is on the basis of an alternative system of valuation or loyalty which is held with passion.

To say that all men have value centers and causes is to move beyond the question *whether* men should worship to the question *what* men should worship. This question is characteristically Hebrew in origin. All men have gods of one sort or another; atheism in the sense of non-worship is impossible: "To deny the reality of a supernatural being called God is one thing; to live without confidence in some center of value and without loyalty to a cause is another." [10]

Niebuhr believes that worship for Western man most frequently takes one of two forms. The first is a kind of polytheism in which men relate themselves alternatively to numerous centers of value—each absolute in the moment of its claim upon the self. The second is a form of henotheism in which men worship the social groupings to which they belong, thus finding their meaning as human beings in relationship to their membership in the group. This second form of worship is perhaps the more typical because it expresses greater coherence. The first is likely to result from the disintegration of a social faith. Social faith can, of course, take the form of loyalty to nation, to family, to race, to clan, to class, even to humanity as a whole (in rare instances). But characteristic of such social faith is that all things are considered good or evil insofar as they reflect the good of and for the group. Loyalty and love is inclusive of membership in the group, although those persons and things outside the bounds of the social loyalty have no claim upon the self. Similarly, feelings of holiness attach to whatever expresses the inner being of the group. Conscience becomes the voice of internalized social values and mores.[11] When this or that form of society fails as god, it is most likely to be replaced by a multiplicity of gods:

When confidence in nation or other closed society is broken, men who must live by faith take recourse to multiple centers of value and scatter their loyalties among many causes. When the half-gods go the minimal gods arrive.[12]

Each is made absolute in the moment our attention is directed toward it, but each absolute gives way in turn to some new absolute as the self moves restlessly from one value center to another after abandoning the quest for a coherent, integrating center of meaning.

Contrasted with these two forms of worship, henotheism and polytheism, is "radical monotheism," the form of worship to which the Christian faith essentially bears witness. Radical monotheism will not settle for worship of any aspect of being which excludes other aspects.

For radical monotheism the value-center is neither closed society nor the principle of such a society but the principle of being itself; its reference is to no one reality among the many but to One beyond all the many, whence all the many derive their being, and by participation in which they exist. As faith, it is reliance on the source of all being for the significance of the self and of all that exists. It is the assurance that because I am, I am valued, and because you are, you are beloved, and because whatever is has being, therefore it is worthy of love. . . . It is not a relation to any finite, natural or supernatural, value-center that confers value on self and some of its companions in being, but it is value relation to the One to whom all being is related.[13]

This identification of the source of being with the source of value (the identification of the center of value with whatever is responsible for all being) finds theological expression in the identification of God as Creator with God as Redeemer or as God of grace. "As faith reliance," Niebuhr continues, "radical monotheism depends absolutely and assuredly for the worth of the self on the same principle by which it has being; and since that principle is the same by which all things exist it accepts the value of whatever is." [14]

This does not mean that all finite things are to be valued equally because they have being—such as the notion that a tree is equal in value to a person because both have being. Relative valuations may indeed establish the greater or lesser goodness of this or that object. But it is supremely important to recognize that such valuations are *relative*. Only the source of being is absolute, and the value of all things is relative to being itself. Radical monotheism thus "dethrones all absolutes short of the principle of being itself." [15] A clear implication of this position is that no manifestation of being itself may be accorded the position of being itself as center of value and meaning without unfaithfulness to all the rest of being which has been excluded. This is, I assume, another way of saying that God transcends every one of his manifestations; including, presumably, his manifestation in the form of theological conceptions by his creatures. This does not require belief that relative manifestations of God are erroneous or valueless. It is, rather, to say that while the relative manifestations of God all point to God, God is still greater.

Richard Niebuhr himself applies this criticism of absolutes even to the church whenever the church is willing to identify God directly and absolutely with a loyalty that is more limited than being itself. It is comparatively common for polytheism or henotheism to masquerade in the clothing of Western religion, but this does not change or sanctify such forms of worship. Whenever Christianity is used simply to undergird national patriotism or whenever it is used to sanctify economic interests it is likely that radical monotheism has succumbed to one of the other forms of faith. That Christianity has often been used for such purposes gives substance to those criticisms of Christianity which argue that Christianity *is* a social faith (Durkheim) or class interest (Marx), although Niebuhr would argue that when Christianity is used in this kind of way it ceases to be the Christian faith.

Implicit here is a vigorous critique of one typical source of the denial of religious liberty—that which has generally been identified as Erastianism (the direct use of religious institutions and culture to serve political ends). This critique, moreover, raises serious religious questions concerning the argument from pluralism which was discussed in the preceding chapter. The point is that both Erastianism and pluralism, as discussed before, place the center of value in the political community rather than in being itself. To defend religious liberty for the sake of the welfare and stability of the political community raises serious questions about forms of religion which seem at the time to be contrary to the interests of the political community. For such reasons are prophets stoned in their day.

More broadly, the idea of radical monotheism undercuts all the religious absolutes on whose bases the denial of religious liberty might be founded. Every witness to being itself must be taken seriously, but not to the extent that other witnesses are excluded. At the very least, the idea places every doctrine or creed which is used as an excuse for religious repression on the defensive to show why it is not a form of idolatry; that is, to show why it is not in fact an absolutizing of the relatively good and the relatively true.

A final comment should be made about the general acceptability of the idea of radical monotheism and the corollary applications which have been developed here. Since Niebuhr in formulating a conception of this kind has been working at a theological frontier, the language which he employs may prove disturbing at points to those who do not recognize in it an affirmation of their present beliefs. The idea of "being itself," for instance, can carry overtones of pantheism or of an ontological rationalism which would, in fact, be far removed from Niebuhr's intention. As I understand his formulations, Niebuhr wishes to express a genuinely Christian understanding of God, but to do so he must purify the idea of God of idolatrous elements and witness to the fact that God is always more than anything that can be said about him. Identification of God with being itself suggests the transcendence as well as immanence of God. The term radical monotheism is well chosen and, as we have suggested, it has important implications for the support of religious liberty.

5. The "Protestant Principle" of Paul Tillich

Other theologians could be enlisted in support of a critique of absolutes in the name of the transcendence of God beyond even theology. The list would include most of the younger theologians in the United States. Already Karl Barth, despite an apparently rigid Christology, used that very approach to God in Christ in the dethronement of absolute human claims:

Christian dogmatics will always be a thinking, an investigation and an exposition which are relative and liable to error. Even dogmatics with the best knowledge and conscience can do no more than question after the better and never forget that we are succeeded by other, later men; and he who is faithful in this task will hope that those other, later men may think and say better and more profoundly what we were endeavoring to think and say.[16]

John Bennett quotes this statement and finds it especially remarkable since Barth "is not noted for a lack of confidence in his own theology."

The theologian who has put the matter most clearly and related it most explicitly to Protestantism, however, is Paul Tillich. In his well-known concept of the Protestant principle, Tillich argues that it is "eternal and a permanent criterion of everything temporal." [17] "Everything temporal" is broadly inclusive of every manifestation of truth in the form of idea and of every manifestation of divine grace in objective form.

The Protestant principle, in name derived from the protest of the "protestants" against decisions of the Catholic majority, contains the divine and human protest against any absolute claim made for a relative reality, even if this claim is made by a Protestant church. The Protestant principle is the judge of every religious and cultural reality, including the religion and culture which calls itself "Protestant." [18]

Theologically, the principle derives from the fact that God represents unconditional being, while man is conditioned in his existence. The principle is implicit wherever theologians have recognized that "the history of religion and culture is a history of permanent demonic distortions of revelation and idolatrous confusions of God and man." Where this recognition has been present, therefore, such theologians have "emphasized and re-emphasized the First Commandment, the infinite distance between God and man, and the judgment of the Cross over and against all human possibilities." [19] The Protestant principle finds corresponding philosophical application in the insight that unconditional truth is always beyond the capacity of the mind, even while it stands as hidden criterion of all truth claims. It is for this reason that the element of risk cannot be expunged from the work of philosophy.

The principle is explicitly related to the Protestant Reformation through an application of the classical Reformation emphasis on the doctrine of Justification through Faith. This doctrine, Tillich has written, "refers not only to the religious-ethical but also to the religious-intellectual life. Not only he who is in sin, but also he who is in doubt is justified through faith." [20] The meaning of this is that even the person who doubts God need not be separated from God, because even in his doubt he expresses concern for the truth and faith in its reality. Through this faith and concern, even when expressed paradoxically as doubt, the divine is present and can work to perfect the understanding. Faith of this kind functions as the faith of the morally imperfect person whose faith in goodness makes it possible for the divine to work in him to perfect him morally: "Just as you are justified as a *sinner* (though unjust, you are just), so in the status of *doubt* you are in the status of truth." [21] The reverse corollary of this is that just as a sinner cannot save himself by good works alone,

you cannot reach God by the work of right thinking or by a sacrifice of the intellect or by a submission to strange authorities, such as the doctrines of the church and the Bible. You cannot, and you are not even asked to try it. Neither works of piety nor works of morality nor works of the intellect establish unity with God. They follow from this unity, but they do not make it. They even prevent it if you try to reach it through them.[22]

Therefore, "it is obvious that the Protestant principle cannot admit any identification of grace with a visible reality, not even with the church on its visible side." [23] It is because Protestantism has implicitly accepted this that Protestantism has been able to employ the methods of critical research in the examination of the historical manifestations of its faith, including critical examination of the Holy Scriptures and the church. The complete scientific honesty with which Protesantism permitted exposure of mythical and legendary elements of the Bible has, Tillich claims, "no parallel in other religions." This willingness "is an impressive and glorious vindication of the truth of the Protestant principle." [24] But even if Protestantism, as a historical movement, were to break faith with the Protestant principle, it would constitute a judgment only on Protestantism, not on the principle itself. Tillich considers the latter to be eternal (and even manifest to some degree in other religions) : "Not the Protestant era, but the Protestant principle is everlasting." [25] Recent developments in Roman Catholicism, which are posterior to the latest edition of Tillich's *The Protestant Era,* even invite the speculation that the Protestant principle might find rest within that church after it has fallen into neglect among Protestants. More hopefully still, these devolpments suggest that the principle might contribute to renewal in all branches of the Christian church in our day.

While the Protestant principle thus denies the full identification of the ultimate and the eternal with any tangible, conditioned object, it is important to add that the principle, to Tillich, is not simply a negative one. The negative judgment upon all absolute claims is on behalf of the absolute which lies beyond any of its manifestations. The constructive possibility of Protestantism lies in the power of the New Being as manifested in Jesus as the Christ, a formulation familiar to all students of Tillich. But even this formulation is understood to be symbolic, always pointing beyond itself toward the ultimate ground of all being. Of course, acceptance of the applicable key insights in such ideas as radical monotheism and the Protestant principle by no means commits Christian theology to other aspects of the thought of the theologians with which these ideas are most intimately associated. To repeat, the applicable insight of the Protestant principle is that God is more than his historical manifestations and that even the doubter bears witness to the divine. Here, then, is another decisive criticism of all absolute claims on the basis of which the denial of religious liberty could logically be mounted.

But it is also significant that Tillich has made the additional claim that this insight *belongs to the essential meaning of Protestantism.* If this is true, as I believe it is, then it is here that Protestant Christians may, as Protestants, most fruitfully seek their ground for supporting religious liberty.

On the other hand, Thomas G. Sanders in his study of *Protestant Concepts of Church and State* clearly demonstrates that there has not been any *one* Protestant position on church-state relations. He shows the five main positions which he identifies and explores to be mutually contradictory at important points and, moreover, comprised by schools of thought which are also contradictory at points. Thus, in relation to religious liberty and church-state matters, the emerging Protestant image is one of diversity, not one of unity or integrity. Even to credit the Reformation with belief in religious liberty as a general principle is an act of considerable license. In an interesting comment on the Sanders book, Franklin H. Littell refers to the problem of whether the Reformers really meant to support religious liberty by remarking that "Dr. Sanders breaks through the latter-day filial writing of Lutherans and Calvinists who attribute to the state-church Reformers views which they specifically rejected, and accredit to them the background of American religious liberty and pluralism which they in fact could not have imagined in their wildest nightmares." [26] If this is so, it would seem naïve to speak of *the* Protestant principle and to expect it to support religious liberty when most logically applied. Sanders

himself refers to Tillich's approach rather briskly with
these words:

Following Paul Tillich, many interpreters of Protestantism
hold that its distinguishing characteristic is the "Protestant
principle": an emphasis on the sovereignty of God, in contrast
with the finiteness of human expressions, which leads to a
focus on divine judgment. But clearly, most Protestants would
not agree.[27]

I am not so sure that most Protestants would not agree if
they understood the Protestant principle and its full im
plications. More importantly, even if most would not
agree it is not clear that their disagreement would reflect
the heart of the matter. Even the Reformers, who by the
standard of the Protestant principle unquestionably in-
dulged in various forms of idolatry and cheerfully joined
in the effort to stamp out heresy from their revised perspectives, may not have been acting out of their own deepest,
most basic insights. Similarly, the fact that many white
Christians in Mississippi "would not agree" with the doctrine that race should be of no consequence in the church
as the body of Christ would not set aside the fact that this
is a clear implication of the Christian faith when it is
properly understood and applied. The history of Christian social ethics is replete with contradictions between
more basic doctrine and the principles of policy drawn
from them. Such contradictions can exist even in the
teachings of the same people. Sanders himself remarks
later in his book that the "sense of relativism and self-
criticism inherent within Protestantism may well be the
most important Protestant contribution to church-state
theory." [28]
Whether Protestants have always accepted the Protestant
principle—the record is surely a spotty one—is secondary

to the question whether it represents insight to which Protestants may in a faithful and principled manner repair. The analysis from the perspective of the theologians quoted in this chapter indicates that it does.

6. Some Concluding Reflections

The point I have argued in this chapter, namely, that the Christian and particularly the Christian as Protestant must always be critical of every claim of absolute truth and value, represents one side of a theologically principled Christian basis for religious liberty. Before moving to the other side, some concluding observations might be made in support of this argument.

Any theologian who wishes to defend the absoluteness or completeness of any manifestation of the divine as a basis for social privilege (and for corresponding social disabilities to be inflicted upon alternative claims) has an incredible amount of Christian experience to argue away. He may begin by asserting that, of course, the perfect manifestation of the divine to the Christian is in the life of Jesus Christ. Disregarding what we have already said, including the statement in Mark 10:18 that "no one is good but God alone," he is immediately confronted by various problems. First, how does he know that his own perception of that manifestation is not distorted? If he argues that he is relying upon the perceptions of the most immediate witnesses, how does he know that his own interpretation of their perceptions is not distorted (assuming their perceptions were not in any way faulty—a risky assumption on scriptural grounds and an impossible one in the light of critical study of the Bible)? Or how does he account for the fact that scarcely any two theologians have viewed the reality in precisely the same way? Or how does he explain the fact that he has himself probably changed his mind several times about the inner meaning of that manifestation before arriving at his present viewpoint? Finally, since the manifestation was in living form, how, precisely, does he propose to create a remanifestation in verbal form which will exactly capture the original event so that it can be exactly reexperienced by later Christians across so vast a gulf of time?

Or, viewing the history of the church, how is one to interpret the hideous mistakes which have so often occurred in the name of an absolute claim? The history of heresy is instructive. In large measure the defining of heresy as heresy undoubtedly has reflected the kind of criticism of erroneous absolutes for which we have argued in this chapter. Heretics have often seized upon some one small aspect of the truth and held it with fanatical zeal to the exclusion of all else. But in the criticism of heresy and in the persecution of heretics Christians have so often done violence to that one small aspect of the truth. One thinks of Arius, whose errors largely were based in his concern to defend monotheism, or of Pelagius, whose errors rooted in his concern that Christianity not be destroyed in the antinomian direction. More ironically, one must reflect upon the considerable difficulties experienced by many of the saints (such as St. Francis of Assisi, Joan of Arc, and even Thomas Aquinas) prior to their wider acceptance and canonization. In such cases the time-honored proof text for religious liberty, the parable of the wheat and the tares (Matt. 13:24-30), finds ample illustration. Or one must make note of the shameful rearguard action which many Christians have fought against this or that advance of science at almost every turn in modern history, only to have to swallow their pride, reinterpret their world view, and move on to the next position of defense.

One can reflect with a certain bemusement upon the embarrassments which premature absolutes and certainties have so often occasioned in both Catholic and Protestant circles. Consider the pope, for instance, in the light of the doctrine of infallibility. He wishes to make a pronouncement on a subject important to him, and he wishes to have his words taken seriously. But no sooner has he spoken than the theologians begin to explain the qualifications, the circumstances, the range of applicability, etc. The process quickens as the pronouncement encounters opposition or must be applied to situations which the pope could not have anticipated. He would need to return centuries later to discover what he had *really* meant! One can think with similar bemusement of the absolute certainties which gave meaning and purpose to people in the small "Bible-belt" Protestant communities of mid-America, where so many were so sure that election of the first Roman Catholic to the presidency in 1960 would mean turning the nation over to the pope. It must be added, of course, that in such communities, as in Roman Catholicism, radical monotheism and the Protestant principle have not been without their witnesses.

A final observation is necessary. I noted earlier Tillich's point that it was the Protestant principle which made it possible for Protestant scholars to engage in biblical criticism in good conscience. This is both true and important. But it should be remembered additionally that the results of that study and the other forms of scientific study of religion have enormous significance in the actual exposure of the relativity of absolute claims for the historical manifestations of religion. The scientific study of the Bible has exposed such absolutes as doctrines of verbal inerrancy. The sociology of religion has exposed the relativity of claims regarding the absolute sanctity of religious institutions. The psychology of religion has shed great light on the psychological bases of religious fanaticism. Anthropological and sociological study has suggested functional parallels between different religious systems and the possibility that much "religious" behavior is actually behavior on the basis of less ultimate forms of motivation. The work of the sciences is also a reminder of the common theme of most epistemological work in philosophy since Hume and Kant, namely that it is not possible to say with certainty that one *knows* anything to be true unless it is a formal truth, such as in logic and mathematics. This has suggested the corresponding importance of faith in every experience of truth and value.

I am well aware that all the academic disciplines from which data critical of religious absolutes can be drawn also exhibit tendencies toward the erection of absolutes which, in turn, require criticism. But the results of several generations of critical work in the scientific and philosophical disciplines help to explain why contemporary students and intellectuals are so frequently disdainful of religious absolutes. In this, whether consciously or unconsciously, they may be bearing partial witness to the Christian understanding that God is more than anything we can know about him.

NOTES

[1] *Religious Liberty* (New York: G. P. Putnam's Sons, 1912), tr. J. Parker Heyes, p. 19.

[2] *Church, State, and Freedom* (Boston: Beacon Press, 1953), p. 6.

[3] Quoted by Wilber G. Katz, "The Case for Religious Liberty," in *Religion in America* (New York: Meridian Books, 1958), p. 113. Commenting on these same passages, Dean Walter G. Muelder has suggested that "it may be that he is in substantial error in relating freedom to skepticism in either or both of these traditions [Protestant dissent and secular humanism]. The problems of power and human nature are, in my view, closer to the historic situation. Freedom

is rooted in a prior covenant with God. Power should not violate free expression of religious obligation" (unpublished lecture, 1962). Dean Muelder's point seems well founded with two qualifications: first, the difficulties suggested in the preceding chapter in the discussion of spiritual dignity and freedom as a sole basis for religious liberty, and second, the fact that the "prior covenant with God" derives its privileged character in large part precisely because its content and modes of expression may not infallibly be predetermined. If this were not the case, outsiders might be tempted to distinguish between "authentic" prior covenants with God and "false" prior covenants with God. The contention of the present chapter is that Protestant faith does not permit certainty in making such distinctions, a view with which I believe Dean Muelder would concur.

⁴ *The Nature and Destiny of Man* (New York: Charles Scribner's Sons, 1943), II, 213 ff.

⁵ *Ibid.*, p. 214.

⁶ *Ibid.*, p. 231.

⁷ "The Theological Basis of Religious Liberty," *loc. cit.*

⁸ *Ibid.*, p. 39.

⁹ Cf. esp. *Radical Monotheism and Western Culture* (New York: Harper and Brothers, 1960).

¹⁰ *Ibid.*, p. 25.

¹¹ This concept gains rich additional meaning in recent sociological discussions of "reference group" theory, although Niebuhr does not make this connection. In general, reference group theory postulates that persons derive their principal valuations and views of reality from the groups with which they identify themselves most completely. Views and valuations, thus, are held to be related to human needs for social approval and love, and the conscience expresses in part the unconscious judgments which the self makes as to the social acceptability of this or that line of action. Refinements of reference group theory comprehend that primary group identifications need not be physically or chronologically immediate. Cf. Robert K. Merton, *Social Theory and Social Structure* (3rd ed. rev.; Glencoe, Ill.: The Free Press, 1957), pp. 225-86.

¹² *Radical Monotheism and Western Culture*, p. 28.

¹³ *Ibid.*, p. 32.

¹⁴ *Ibid.*, p. 33.

¹⁵ *Ibid.*, p. 37.

¹⁶ *Dogmatics in Outline* (New York: Philosophical Library, 1949), p. 11, quoted by John C. Bennett, *Christians and the State* (New York: Charles Scribner's Sons, 1958), p. 139. Despite the fact that this is a quite characteristic statement by Barth, this eminent theologian may not be used in support of the thesis of this chapter with-

out considerable qualification. Note, for example, the following statement which also appears in *Dogmatics in Outline:* "The truth of Jesus Christ is not one truth among others; it is *the* truth, the universal truth that creates all truth as surely as it is the truth of God, the *prima veritas* which is also the *ultima veritas*" (p. 26). I think it fair to say that Barth is anxious to preserve both the full certitude of faith and God's transcendence of everything human. Cf. also his statement that "The revelation of God, in which man's fulfilment of the true knowledge of God takes place, is the disposition of God in which He acts towards us as the same triune God that He is in Himself, and in such a way that, although we are men and not God, we receive a share in the truth of His knowledge of Himself. Certainly it is the share which He thinks proper and which is therefore suitable for us." *Church Dogmatics,* II, Part 1, 51.

[17] *The Protestant Era,* tr. by James Luther Adams (Chicago: The University of Chicago Press, 1948), p. xii.

[18] *Ibid.,* p. 163.

[19] *Ibid.,* p. xxviii.

[20] *Ibid.,* p. xiv.

[21] *Ibid.,* p. xv.

[22] *Ibid.*

[23] *Ibid.,* p. xxi.

[24] *Ibid.,* p. xxvii.

[25] *Ibid.,* p. xxix.

[26] Review in *A Journal of Church and State,* VI, No. 3 (1964), 368.

[27] *Protestant Concepts of Church and State,* p. 3.

[28] *Ibid.,* p. 284.

IV

Protestant Faith as Expectancy

The case against absolute identification of truth or salvation with visible realities seems clear enough in Protestant perspective. The case is buttressed, moreover, by epistemological analysis and the vast historical evidence of human fallibility. Nor is there much question of the relevance of this case to the problem at hand. If truth and salvation cannot be known absolutely as visible realities, neither can they be protected with assurance as visible realities. The basis for denial of religious liberty, accordingly, dissolves. A serious problem remains, however, in that this negative support for religious liberty seems exactly parallel to a purely skeptical approach. The theologian must therefore inquire whether we are here attempting to base religious liberty upon skepticism or a flabby equating of all religions as equally true or equally false—thereby undercutting confidence in the claims of the Christian faith.

1. Beyond Skepticism and Relativism

Theologians have understandably been reluctant to pay that kind of price for religious liberty. The Christian faith is not merely tentative. It is not apologetic in its confrontation of other religions or of the world in general, for the Christian faith is a definite view of reality. It asserts the meaning and value of life, and in the face of all that denies life, the Christian is properly dogmatic in his claims. In such a dogmatic spirit, Christians of many generations have challenged evil face to face. With notable courage they have confronted suffering and even the prospect of martyrdom. And they have brought a saving perspective to diseased civilization. Twentieth-century illustrations of the resisting, restorative, and creative powers of Christian faith abound. But such illustrations could not have been founded upon a thoroughgoing skepticism.

One of the striking features in A. F. Carrillo de Albornoz' summary of ecumenical discussions on the theological basis of religious liberty is the explicit rejection of skepticism by most of the theologians who have participated in these discussions. This rejection would probably extend to a certain unhappiness with the point of view of the preceding chapter in the present volume. Dr. Carrillo has summarized the consensus in this way:

The Christian notion of religious liberty by no means includes any element of indifferentism, relativism or syncretism. Christians consider God's revelation as the absolute and unique truth, but demand religious liberty for all, including erring men, *in spite of that absoluteness*.[1]

And, at another point in his discussion, he remarks that

one of the reasons which lead some theologians to look for the Christian basis of religious liberty in the limitations of civil power is their reluctance to accept the view that religious freedom can be derived from faith. As they say, "tolerance cannot be derived from faith, *because the Christian faith is absolute truth*.[2]

"Every Christian," he continues,

would agree with the opinion that every inclination towards a recognition of two or more possibilities of truth must be avoided and that, therefore, we cannot demand freedom of religion based on our religious doubts. . . . Every social religious liberty based on relativism of the truth or on practical indifference concerning it is not a religious freedom to be asked for by Christians. The consideration of the weakness and fallibility of human thought (which should be accepted, if correctly understood) can be the motivation for some individual or social "tolerance" towards the errors or mistakes of others; but this should never be the theological basis for the complete social liberty of all religions, as if all (including the Christian one) were more or less equivalent concerning the revelation of the divine truth. This would be syncretism or relativism; never Christian insight.[3]

In evaluating these remarks, it should be remembered that they do not simply reflect Dr. Carrillo's opinion. They represent an important consensus among a large number of the mature theologians who have participated in ecumenical discussion of the subject.

There are good logical, ethical, and theological grounds for rejecting relativism or skepticism.

On *logical* grounds, it has long been observed that a thoroughgoing skepticism is self-undermining. If one cannot know anything for sure, how can one know *that?* And if one makes an exception of the knowledge claim that all knowledge is relative or uncertain, what is the basis of that exception? This logical problem attaches to the claim of a

Protestant critique of all absolute identification of truth or means of salvation with visible realities. The question is, have we made an absolute of the critique itself, or is the critique based on an absolute of some other sort? If so, or if it is, why have we exempted that absolute from the critique? And could not that absolute form the basis for a new intolerance—namely, an intolerance of the intolerant?

The *ethical* problem is that skepticism or relativism undercuts identification of the good in human experience and weakens action on its behalf. A generation which is skeptical about Christianity might be willing enough to criticize the "pretension" of churches in sending out missionaries to disturb the harmonies of alien cultures. But that same generation rises up in wrath and indignation at the spectacle of racial discrimination or Fascism and renders quite absolute judgments against such social evils—despite the fact that racial discrimination and Fascism also seem good to some people. Ironically, it would even seem inconsistent to criticize a missionary-sending church on relativistic grounds, for if missionary sending is an aspect of the cultural value system of the church, mustn't this be accepted by a relativist as "just one of those things"? As a matter of fact, any conclusion which is reached in the present study which has the effect of relativizing religious or ethical truth claims must be examined scrupulously in the light of, say, Mississippi. To what extent am I, as a Christian who considers the racial valuations and practices of that society repugnant and wrong, willing to grant them a possibility of truth? That is a hard question, but one which cannot honestly be avoided. If it is answered by giving up the basis for judging goodness and identifying justice and injustice, it may lead to cynicism. If it is answered by giving up the Protestant critique of absolutes, it may destroy the argument advanced in the preceding chapter.

124

The *theological* problem is that there could be no basis for Christian faith if skepticism reigned and all truth claims were reduced to relativity and indifference. Indeed, there is a sense in which theology demands a certain degree of intolerance, not necessarily of persons but of ideas which are taken to be wrong. As G. K. Chesterton put it, "Tolerance is the virtue of people who don't believe anything." [4] Christians *do* believe something, or they would not be Christians. Moreover, mere skepticism may even be a weak basis for religious liberty because it makes high religion more vulnerable to the limited social idols of clan or nation or race—witness the unfortunate history of the Third Reich.

But there is a further dimension to the theological problem.

The approach which was taken in the preceding chapter may have commended itself to some as being, in a sense, both inescapable and at the same time unacceptable. Inescapable because it does indeed convey the Christian's proper humility in the presence of the transcendent God. But unacceptable because it seems to suggest that the Christian life is basically cognitive—which it is not. It is a great deal easier to entertain a certain relativism, even a certain skepticism, regarding the intellectual presentation of Christian doctrine than it is to accept relativism regarding the living reality to which that doctrine points. What is that reality? It is not to be encountered in intellectual assent to correct doctrine, nor certainly in accurate perception of formal or empirical truth; rather, it is in being grasped by the love of God. When Christians speak of this, they do not intend to be abstract. They intend to convey a sense of life which is more than symbolic and more than doctrinal formulation. Moreover, they mean to say that life in the setting of the grace of God is *qualitatively and discernibly different* from life which is alienated from that context. Paul's great letters convey this sense classically. Behind the symbolism, metaphor, and doctrinal formulations, there is an important living theme which has been recovered by Christian thinkers in every age of theological renewal: Man's salvation from sin and death is a gift of the Father's love. It may not be earned through essentially self-seeking works. It is revealed in Christ, by whose death on the cross is conveyed both the depth of the divine love and the ultimate seriousness of sin. Through being grasped by the love of God, man himself receives the capacity to act in loving response—as in a family where children do not mature in goodness until they have a sense of being loved, so it is with man before God. In a sense the portrait is categorical. It suggests an interpretation of the meaning of life itself which cannot entertain even the possibility that its contrasting opposites (lovelessness, hopelessness, selfishness, etc.) have anything positive to offer man. The issue at stake is literally one of life or death. It not only matters, but it matters everything.

I believe that it is this kind of consideration which has drawn a number of thinkers, such as Hendrik Kraemer, into categorical distinctions between "Christian faith" and "religion," the latter including every non-Christian point of view and many so-called Christian ones. "Christian faith" is trustful response to God's free gift of love. "Religion" is man's *search* for the ultimate; it is something which is essentially man-made. If one sees these distinctions solely in terms of cognitive claims regarding the nature of reality there appears to be an arrogance about them which is at least partly missing when one perceives them in terms of personal, existential life. The religion of the Buddhist, for instance, is not despised because it is, speculatively speaking, considered to be an inferior philosophical description of reality. It is seen, rather, in terms of whether the Buddhist as a person is able to encounter the abundant life in Buddhism.

Conversely, it must be said that the more latitudinarian views associated with William Ernest Hocking, Arnold Toynbee, and others derive largely from their more distinctively cognitive approach to world religions. Cognitively speaking, there is great insight to be found wherever human culture has produced thinkers, and men of the stature of Hocking and Toynbee have been big enough to recognize this even from vast cultural distances. Accordingly and understandably they have been impatient with what could appear to be the arrogant small-mindedness of Christian theologians who seem to clutch their fragments of the wider truth within the security of a religious ghetto. Christian theology, however, must press the point that its interest is not solely cognitive but that it pertains to the salvation of man's whole nature.

How should these logical, ethical, and theological points be understood in the light of a Protestant interpretation of Christian faith?

2. The Positive Basis of Protestant Criticism

If it is to avoid the logical problem, every criticism must be based on some positive assumption which is not itself held to be problematical. In various ways, this is clearly recognized by the theologians referred to in the preceding chapter in support of the Protestant criticism of absolutes. Reinhold Niebuhr locates it in the categorical assertion of man's self-transcendence. H. Richard Niebuhr makes positive assertions about being itself, to which man must relate himself in monotheistic worship. Paul Tillich in his writing on the Protestant principle locates the positive, constructive element in "the New Being manifest in Jesus as the Christ." None of these theologians would happily term himself a skeptic or a relativist, although each has contributed to skepticism and relativism regarding identification of divine truth in objective form. The formal relationship between criticism of all relative manifestations of truth and the absolute basis for that criticism may be established without considering such formulas to be inconsistent. Formally speaking, as Tillich has remarked in one of his writings, "What is true . . . of all knowledge cannot be true of the knowledge of knowledge, otherwise it would cease to have universal significance." [5] There is a difference between specific truth claims and acknowledgment of the possibility of truth. The latter is absolute in its claim, while the former is relative. This is partly clarified by the definition of truth as correspondence between idea and reality. That reality may be known is a formal assertion which must be made by all who participate in intellectual intercourse. But the truth of any particular truth claim does not follow therefrom. The Protestant faith must bear witness to reality and its knowability, but it also functions in the criticism of every specific truth claim.

Similarly, regarding the ethical problem of identifying and acting upon the good: It is a categorical necessity to affirm the reality of goodness as a precondition to moral experience. But this does not establish the goodness of any particular ethical claim. Absolute ethical relativism is no more possible than epistemological relativism, unless one wishes to abolish man's moral nature altogether (and therewith, it must be added, the significance of human life).

Theologically, moreover, it is one thing to say that the Christian faith is just one more interpretation of life alongside other interpretations which are of equal value. Such relativism would have to be discarded, I believe, even as a precondition for meaningful dialogue among religious viewpoints. It certainly is not consistent with the claims of the Christian faith. But it is quite another thing to say that the Christian faith bears witness to a reality greater than all that the earthen vessels of Christian men, society, and culture can contain. Nor is it necessary, theologically, to deny that God has immediate access to all men and all cultures in ways which it would be blasphemous for a Christian to prejudge. Furthermore, since the Christian faith refers to living relationships, it must be understood that the religious experience of every person (his relationship with God) will be unique, unpredictable, and unrepeatable. Theology, in other words, can bear witness to the Christian view of reality, including the noncognitive issues of sin and salvation to which I have referred above, without having to suggest that reality is limited to our understanding of it.

I believe that the positive basis of the Protestant criticism is most appropriately found in the classical concept of the sovereignty of God. Professor Sanders has pointed out three implications of this doctrine which have important applicability to problems of church-state relationship. These are (1) "that the state may serve as an instrument of God's historical activity," (2) "that the political order is established for particular abiding purposes," and (3) that, "if God is active in political and social institutions, he has a purpose for them which can to some extent be learned." [6] These three implications are clear in their positive affirmation of God's concern for the world and of man's obligation to discover and act upon the will of God if he is to fulfill the intention of human life. A fourth point needs to be added, however, in affirming the transcendence of God above every human conception and enterprise. Man is not God. Man must acknowledge the possibility that his cognitive and moral endeavors may be tainted with error and self-seeking. And even if they are not, man must acknowledge that God is also beyond. It is in the failure to acknowledge the transcendence of God that man falls prey to the idolatries which H. Richard Niebuhr has discussed. Indeed, there is a curious sense in which the failure to acknowledge the sovereign transcendence of God serves to relativize God. That is, when we absolutize the relative, paradoxically, we relativize the absolute. Where the finite is invested with ultimacy, the infinite is lost. This does not mean that the finite may not symbolically represent the infinite. But when the symbol is mistaken for the reality it symbolizes, it stands as a barrier between the self and that reality.

This should suggest, incidentally, the importance of mystery in Christian faith. While the idea of mystery has been used to cloud issues which were not so mysterious and to preclude valuable researches to broaden understanding of what was previously mysterious, it is appropriately recognized as a corollary of the sovereignty of God that there should be mystery as well as disclosure in God's relationships with his subjects. The Christian holds that God has disclosed himself in Jesus Christ and the Christian lives in daily expectation of God's further disclosure of his nature and purposes. But this should not lead to Christian arrogance about perfect understanding of God any more than the continual progress of science leads any competent scientist to expect suddenly to become aware of all the secrets of the physical universe.[7] The more appropriate Christian response is one of humility, diligence, and expectancy.

All this should lead us to take both truth and error and good and evil with maximum seriousness. Truth is taken seriously because it is recognized that idea can correspond

to reality. Error is taken seriously because it is recognized
that it may not and because it is understood that reality is
always more than idea. Good is taken seriously because it is
believed that God is good and that man may respond to
God's purposes. Sin is taken seriously because it is known
that man may also rebel against those purposes. In the
language of Pascal, "every single thing is partly true and
partly false," and "both truth and goodness" are possessed
by human beings "only mixed with falsehood and error." [8]

Why should the Christian ask for more? Is there really
anything about the Christian faith which requires one to
accept either of the false alternatives of knowing everything or of being skeptical, relativistic, or syncretistic? Can
we not be fully grateful for the revelation which God has
given us and which we, indeed, may correct and understand progressively more each passing year—and at the
same time acknowledge that there may be still more to
God's self-disclosure? As a five-year-old child one may know
decisively true things about one's parents and their love,
but the passing years bring new disclosures. Never does
one know everything about them. Is the Christian claim
not of this order—remembering always that the distance
between God and man is vastly greater than that of parent
and child, just as the love of God is understood to be vastly
more intimate and tender?

3. The Protestant Expectancy

Despite the existence of error and sin, the Protestant expectancy is that we may encounter the activity of God
wherever we turn. This is part of the insight which Richard Niebuhr has caught in his concept of radical monotheism. There is no realm of existence which is secular in
the sense of being outside the framework of God's activity,
just as there is no aspect of existence which is sacred in

the sense of completely encompassing all of God. This is why it must be considered an act of idolatry to take some one aspect of the activity of God and use it to deny all other aspects. Accordingly, Christians are sensitive to the ubiquity of God's workings, in nature as well as in history. This is why Christians approach every encounter with other human beings sensitive to God at work in the other and most desirous of relating to the other on that plane.

In Protestant tradition the immediate access of every person to God was emphasized most by Quakers with their doctrine of the inner light, by Baptists who emphasized individual responsibility and the Holy Spirit, and by Luther, of course, with his doctrine of the priesthood of all believers.[9] Despite his failure to think and act always in the expectancy of finding God at work in others, Luther bore striking witness to that expectancy by reminding his readers that God "once spoke through the mouth of an ass." "Therefore," he concluded, "no man is to be despised, however humble he may be." At the same time Luther pointed out that God "permitted the highest angel to fall from heaven; therefore, no man is to be trusted, no matter how wise, holy, or great he may be." Accordingly, "one should rather give a hearing to all, and wait to see through which one of them God will speak and act." [10] This is in the spirit of Protestant expectancy.

The most obvious theological objection to this concept of Protestant expectancy derives from a radical doctrine of the Fall. The objection may be expressed in the following way: Both man and creation need to be understood as fallen, even though God is not by definition excluded from any man or any aspect of creation. Man and creation are under the power of the denial of God. Only through *redeemed* creation is God's activity to be sought. Specifically, God is not to be encountered at work outside the context of Christian faith except in and through the encounter of Christian faith with fallen man and creation.

But few Christians would want to accept all the implications of so radical a doctrine of the Fall, for to do so one would have to exclude God as the source of positive being except where this could be related to Christian redemption (that is, redemption through encounter with the Christian tradition). In other words, every expression of love, of truth, goodness, and beauty encountered outside the environs of Christian tradition would have to be attributed to powers which resist God. God could not be viewed as working even in a preparatory way to lead creation toward redemption. The sheer arrogance of so flat a denial of the power of God, even though it may certainly be encountered here and there in the history of Christian doctrine (and even though it may point toward powers of evil which must be taken seriously), is one reason why some have been alienated from the positive witness of Christian faith.[11]

It must be added that even though the conception we are discussing here has been called the "Protestant Expectancy" and even though this conception is considered to be an aspect of "Protestant Faith," Roman Catholicism has often borne witness to it to at least a limited degree. A recent illustration is provided by the "Declaration on the Relation of the Church to Non-Christian Religions," which was adopted by the Second Vatican Council and proclaimed by Pope Paul VI in October, 1965. In the midst of an appreciative listing of the good points in such non-Christian religions as Buddhism, Islam, and Judaism, the Declaration includes the following significant paragraphs:

The Catholic Church rejects nothing which is true and holy in these religions. She looks with sincere respect upon those

133

ways of conduct and of life, those rules and teachings which, though differing in many particulars from what she holds and sets forth, nevertheless often reflect a ray of that Truth which enlightens all men. Indeed, she proclaims and must ever proclaim Christ, "the way, the truth, and the life" (John 14: 6), in whom men find the fullness of religious life, and in whom God has reconciled all things to Himself (cf. 2 Cor. 5:18-19).

The Church therefore has this exhortation for her sons: prudently and lovingly, through dialogue and collaboration with the followers of other religions, and in witness of Christian faith and life, acknowledge, preserve, and promote the spiritual and moral goods found among these men, as well as the values in their society and culture.

Such a statement must be viewed as heartening by those, Protestants and Catholics alike, who take the Protestant expectancy seriously.

While the negative work of criticism of exclusive identifications of God with visible realities is obviously supportive of religious liberty by weakening the basis for religious persecution, it remains to be asked whether the positive basis of that critique and the Protestant expectancy toward which it points also contribute to religious liberty or whether they weaken it. The reader should recall here Dr. Carrillo's assertion that "Christians consider God's revelation as the absolute and unique truth, but demand religious liberty for all, including erring men, in spite of that absoluteness." [12]

Against this view, it must be said that Christians demand religious liberty for all, not only because of the element of skepticism implicit in their critique of all claims, but also on the basis of their own absolute claim. If God is possibly at work in all persons, there is expectancy regarding the capacity of every man to bear a unique witness to the character of being. In other words, every man may well be the bearer of something of value which will be lost if he is denied the right to make his contribution. Moreover, God will have been frustrated in his intention to communicate through the man who is silenced by his fellows. In this sense, Christian discussion of "religious freedom" may be radically reconstructed when Christians come to realize that *they are not so much talking about the freedom of man to be or not be "religious" as they are talking about the freedom of God.* Will God be left free to speak to and through all men? Or will Christians, idolatrously sure that this or that interpretation of God's nature and will represents the only possibility, make it humanly impossible for God to speak through the unlikely, the slightly off-beat, or even through those who deny him? While the element of skepticism inherent in the Christian critique of absolutes is half of the Protestant basis for religious liberty, the Protestant expectancy of God's activity is the other half. The latter is the more decisive, indeed, because in its light religious liberty is not only logical, but it matters.

The heart of the problem really is whether religious liberty is to be sought for all as an act of charity or whether it is to be sought for the sake of charity *and* the word of God which is potentially on the lips of every man—not just because he is a potential convert, but because God is deemed to have access to him.

These observations require that explicit attention be paid to those forms of religious witness which seem most alien to the Christian faith or even most hostile to God.

4. The Question of Heresy and Error

The Protestant expectancy is that there is enough redeeming good or possibility of good in every religious expression to warrant a policy of public protection.[13] Can that expectancy survive close examination of heresy (or mistaken interpretations of Christian faith) and error (or faulty perceptions of truth in general) ? This, after all, is the main problem of religious liberty: is heresy or error to be suppressed or merely tolerated because its results are objectively harmful, or is it to be treated expectantly for the sake of possible good which it may contain? In facing this question, one's answer must encompass not only the classical Christian heresies, but such modern rivals of Christian faith as Communism, Fascism, scientism, secular humanism, hedonism, racism, and nationalism in addition, of course, to the other great world religions and many minor and more primitive ones. Offering defense of the Protestant expectancy in the face of such an array of mixed truth and positive mischief may be rugged business, but it is necessary if the perspective advanced here is the correct one.

Several things can be said which apply more or less to most kinds of heresy or error.

1. It needs to be noted that *the heretic or person in error may very well be more in earnest, more alive religiously, more willing to face important ultimate issues than a person who is willing to conform to this or that orthodox creed simply in order to avoid trouble.* Heretics have often been willing to suffer for their beliefs. Their very earnestness of conviction may be an important witness to reality, as Tillich has suggested intriguingly in his application of the principle of justification by faith to the situation of serious doubt. He who is earnestly wrong may be closer to reality (and therefore to God) than he who is complacently correct in his doctrine. Walter Nigg has expressed this possibility somewhat ecstatically in his introduction to a study of heresy in Christian history:

The heretic has this in common with the prophet and the saint: that he is religiously alive, filled with Christian dynamism, and prepared to sacrifice everything for his faith. He is the extreme antithesis of the indifferentist, or of the person whose central concern is ecclesiastical diplomacy and policy. The heretic is in deadly earnest; he does not straddle the fence. He courageously accepts the consequences of his actions. His fervor can teach us the meaning of loyalty to truth. We may even say that the heretic embodies the religious spirit in concentrated form. The principles of Christianity take first place with him; to these he subordinates everything else. This statement applies to almost all the significant figures among the heretics.[14]

While some heretics have also exhibited the more regrettable marks of fanaticism (as Nigg concedes, some have been "pathological troublemakers"), there is enough truth in the more generous appraisal to record as a valuable contribution the spirit and devotion of many who have otherwise been in error.

2. *Time may reverse our appraisal of what is true or false, or it may show that what appeared to be error really is a higher truth.* Let no Christian suppose that Christian revelation has ended this possibility. Most of us would say that Paul grasped the essence of that revelation, yet in matters of social policy he was not far ahead of his time. Consider, for example, his apparent support of slavery as an institution, his discussion of the comparative roles of the sexes in marriage, his remarks on tonsorial proprieties in the church fellowship ("Does not nature itself teach you that for a man to wear long hair is degrading to him, but if a woman has long hair, it is her pride?" I Cor. 11:14-15a), and the comparatively unrelieved conservatism of his doctrine of the state. Christian history is abundantly peopled by even more dramatic illustrations of error orig-

137

inally mistaken for truth and of truth originally mistaken for error. Commenting on this, Nigg has written that

> only too often in ecclesiastical history the profounder conception has been worsted because the time was not yet ripe for it. Victory must not be identified with truth! In the course of history, movements representing a false claim to truth have frequently won at least initial victories, and much time has passed before defeated men have been vindicated. . . . Out of the history of the heretics there emerges a buried truth which unexpectedly begins to glow with new radiance.[15]

The difficulties of novel understanding are particularly noteworthy in the fields of natural science and social policy. Most of the outstanding achievements of science have initially elicited the warm opposition of a mistaken church. Advances in democratic political and economic understanding have likewise drawn the fire of mistaken Christians, of which there are few better illustrations than the famous (and ironically named) "Syllabus of Errors" of Pope Pius IX and the rearguard engagement fought against social justice in the United States by Protestant "rugged individualism." Christians cannot know in advance which of the cross-firing ideas and opinions are destined to be recognized as a higher truth, but the reception given to new insight in the past might well contribute greater humility on the one hand and greater expectancy on the other. The parable of the wheat and the tares (Matt. 13:24-30, 36-43) is a useful biblical symbol for this spirit and one which, not surprisingly, has buttressed Christian discussion of religious liberty for many centuries.[16]

3. A largely erroneous view may contain important aspects of the truth which need new emphasis. Heresies are often of this order because the error itself may result from overemphasis upon some point which the church has previously neglected. Pelagianism, for instance, emphasized the importance of man's own ethical effort and striving to the neglect of the role of divine grace (a neglect which Christian theology cannot overlook). If Pelagianism were rejected in its entirety, however, the result would be total rejection of man's own ethical effort. Some interpreters of contemporary Communism have similarly pointed out that many of its emphases represent points of Christian affirmation—despite the distortions found in its over-optimistic doctrine of man, its repudiation of the state as a permanently necessary aspect of social life, and its atheism. If Communism were simply and completely rejected as such, its critique of exploitation and its witness for economic justice would have to be disavowed also. In his classic defense of liberty, John Stuart Mill expressed the point in his remark that

though silenced opinion be an error, it may, and very commonly does, contain a portion of the truth; and since the general or prevailing opinion on any subject is rarely or never the whole truth, it is only the collision of adverse opinion that the remainder of the truth has a chance of being supplied.[17]

Curiously, even hedonism may appear as a corrective of an overexaggerated asceticism which does violence to man's created nature.

4. Error may stimulate the clarification of the truth. Again, as Mill emphasizes,

the peculiar evil of silencing the expression of an opinion is, that it is robbing the human race: posterity as well as the existing generation; those who dissent from the opinion, still more than those who hold it. If the opinion is right, they are deprived of the opportunity of exchanging error for truth; if wrong, they lose, what is almost as great a benefit, the

139

clearer perception and livelier impression of truth, produced by its collision with error.[18]

This "collision" with an opposing point of view is considered by Mill to be so important that "if opponents of all important truths do not exist, it is indispensable to imagine them, and supply them with the strongest arguments which the most skillful devil's advocate can conjure up." For the Christian, the acid test of this proposition might well be supplied by atheism. It hardly seems possible for a Christian to be an atheist.[19] But the history of atheism affords rich insight into the triviality with which many Christians have conceived of God, precisely because atheism has so often been based upon conceptions of God which it felt it had to reject. Atheism, therefore, has been useful at least in clarifying what God *is not*. That is, it has helped to expose idolatries. One may be impressed when one reads of Russian cosmonauts holding press conferences to announce (gravely) that they have not encountered God in their journeys through the heavens. The impressive thing is their assumption that the non-visibility of God is supposed to indicate that God is not real. Paradoxically, this kind of "evidence" of the nonexistence of God might indeed have efficacy in purifying the more simplistic theological views of some who suppose that God is a visible object along with other visible objects. Similarly, Unitarianism in its traditional form reflected protest not simply against the doctrine of the Trinity (which it may have misunderstood) but against a supposed tritheism or belief in three gods. Not surprisingly, Unitarians were considered atheists by many, and this fact doubtless drove some to atheism because they could not in honesty entertain a tritheistic view of God. The Christian may consider it a pity that some people never move beyond atheism into a richer understanding of God, but it is undoubtedly true that atheism has stimulated Christians to find a more refined understanding of what they mean by God. If some insist upon throwing out the baby with the bath water, as the popular expression goes, it may stimulate others to distinguish more carefully between baby and water. Such a contribution is by no means to be despised.

5. *Persons or groups who expound error which is unredeemed by even this much value, may have important contributions to make in other areas which would be disrupted if they were prevented from bearing witness to their mistaken beliefs.* Michael Servetus, who was tried as a heretic in Calvin's Geneva and burned at the stake, affords an interesting illustration (even though few would agree with Calvin today that Servetus' religious views were so totally without value taken by themselves). The interesting thing is that Servetus had already made signal contributions to the growth of physiological science and might conceivably have made many more had he survived. He is credited, among other things, with discovery of the pulmonary circulation of the blood. The stake at Champel thus deprived mankind of a great talent.

6. *Heresy may reflect social interests which have been overlooked but which must be considered in the interests of justice.* The interaction between "heretical" movements and social discontent is a striking phenomenon. Persecution of such movements, indeed, may reflect the unrecognized vested interests of the persecutor which are more important to him than defense of the faith. Or religious establishments may simply neglect to probe deeply enough beneath what are taken to be heretical expressions in an effort to examine nonreligious causes which may be more significant. Historically, the Lollards, the Hussites, the

141

Albigensians, the French weavers, the German peasants, the English "Diggers" and "Levelers," all reflect a combination of religious ideas with social discontent. Religious schism has often been rooted in sociological, rather than theological, causes, although it may express itself entirely in terms of the latter.[20] In our own day, those who simply take Communism or the resurgence of Asian religions at face value will miss much of the true significance of such ideological and religious phenomena. Communism manifestly represents social forces which are broader than its ideological appeal. The resurgence of Buddhism, Hinduism, Islam, etc., is at least partly due to a reaction against Western colonialism and the desire of ancient societies to reassert their cultural dignity. Even Fascism, deplorable a force though it has been in the past two generations, is largely reflective of social discontent which is quite overlooked by those who concentrate solely upon criticism of its idolatrous forms of ideology. It is commonplace today to relate the rise of Hitler to hurt national pride and the crushing reparations thrust upon Germany by the victorious allies following World War I; but it is grand tragedy that these forces were not anticipated creatively by more enlightened people. Even racism and extreme reactionary movements (such as the Ku Klux Klan, the John Birch Society, the Black Muslims, and McCarthyism on the American scene) suggest the need for deeper analysis than simple dismissal of such modern heresies—heresies though they undoubtedly are.[21] All of this is to say that erroneous views may represent and communicate social realities which the Christian must strive to understand.

7. Finally, *the open expression of error may be useful in checking a premature consensus.* To say that man is social and in dialogue with his fellowman is to say that he is also in search of agreement or consensus. There would

be little point in the expression of religious views if the
objective were not to seek agreement upon those views.
Hopefully men enter into dialogue expecting correction
and clarification of their previous views, but in any case
they seek agreement. This is the basis upon which a church
is conceivable. The Catholic principle, fully consistent
with Christian faith, is that Christians should be at one in
their faith so far as possible and that they should be in
dialogue on those points where they find oneness elusive.
More generally, every society (insofar as it is civilized) is
likewise based upon some consensus and upon dialogue
with respect to other points. In this sense, the notion of a
"public philosophy" is not as impossible as some Christian
thinkers believe. But the very tendencies which drive a
society or church toward consensus may make the temptation overwhelming to take shortcuts to unity by imposing
a consensus which does not (at least not *yet*) accord with
everybody's considered judgment. In this situation, the
expression of dissent—no matter how much it is in error
or even how irresponsible it may be—at least saves society
from the illusion of unanimity. Since perfect consensus is
scarcely imaginable, particularly in view of the emerging
worldwide civilization, every consensus must remain at
least somewhat open to new clarification. Error, thus, can
serve as a symbol for yet undiscovered truth.

Much of what has been said here about consensus would
be accepted by John Courtney Murray, whose conception
of civilization in dialogue is full of important insight. At
one point, however, he would probably want to disagree
with what has been said here. Sincere error, responsibly
expressed, has possibilities in the dialogue which he would
not find in insincere, irresponsible communication. The
latter is a form of barbarism; and modern society for all

its appearance of civility is peopled to a regrettable degree with barbarians.

The barbarian need not appear in bearskins with a club in hand. He may wear a Brooks Brothers suit and carry a ball-point pen with which to write his advertising copy. In fact, even beneath the academic gown there may lurk a child of the wilderness, untutored in the high tradition of civility. . . . This is perennially the work of the barbarian, to undermine rational standards of judgment, to corrupt the inherited intuitive wisdom by which the people have always lived, and to do this not by spreading new beliefs but by creating a climate of doubt and bewilderment in which clarity about the larger aims of life is dimmed and the self-confidence of the people is destroyed.[22]

Presumably Fr. Murray would be reluctant to indulge the "expectancy" of God speaking in any important way through the barbarian. But the barbarism of modern civilization, including the philosophical positivisms and existentialisms to which he apparently makes reference, do at least the service of keeping dialogue real—even if they are not able responsibly to enter therein themselves. Such barbarism may point to ancient truths which have become somewhat unglued and are in need of repair and clarification. It may point also to dehumanizing economic, sociological, or political forces which must be addressed for the sake of the health of persons and of public life. Though negative, such are realities which in the name of God one may not ignore; the barbarian of today, as the Assyrian of old, may be God's messenger of a truth which needs perceptive understanding.

Such are the possibilities even to be found in heresy and error.

The Protestant expectancy, then, is that God may communicate reality to and through man everywhere. If God is sovereign over creation, it is blasphemous to prejudge any human witness to reality, and it is Christian to seek the truth expectantly in and behind all human witnesses to truth. Even error, as we have seen, can point toward truth.

This chapter should not be concluded, however, without yet another reminder that, if one may legitimately expect to encounter some truth in or through all men, one must also expect error and take it seriously. The expectancy of finding truth should not inhibit the Christian from rigorous criticism of error and wrong. Nor should human fallibility and humility lead one to withhold one's criticism. Criticism need not be prejudgment if it is in reaction to what has already been expressed, and it is not presumptuous if it does not seek to silence the other or to break off communication with him. Indeed, the task of the Christian who takes both truth and error, good and evil seriously is to draw into dialogue and responsible relationship persons who have settled for this or that idolatry and to draw into love persons who have given themselves over to hatred, bitterness, and hopelessness.

In the Protestant criticism of idolatry and in the Protestant expectancy there is a principled basis for religious liberty as a social policy which should reassure non-Christians that Christians can be trusted and which should point Christians toward their authentic witness to God.

In order to consider the political meaning of these ideas, it is necessary to examine now the concept of the responsible state in relation to Protestant insight.

NOTES

[1] *The Basis of Religious Liberty,* p. 147 (italics mine).

[2] *Ibid.,* p. 88 (italics mine).

[3] *Ibid.*

[4] Quoted by Reinhold Niebuhr in *The Nature and Destiny of Man,* II, 238.

[5] *The Interpretation of History,* p. 169. Quoted by Reinhold Niebuhr in *The Nature and Destiny of Man,* p. 217.

[6] Sanders, *Protestant Concepts of Church and State,* pp. 8-10.

[7] By using this comparison, I am not suggesting that revelation in the theological sense is the same thing as discovery in the scientific sense. But humility is required of both the Christian and the scientist (or the Christian as scientist) in the face of the yet undisclosed.

[8] Fragment 385, quoted by Walter G. Nigg, *The Heretics* (New York: Alfred A. Knopf, 1962), p. 123.

[9] Cf. the suggestive discussion in Sanders, *Protestant Concepts of Church and State,* pp. 199 ff.

[10] *Luther's Works,* XLV, 121.

[11] The expectancy that God is to be encountered throughout creation, though inconsistent with a radical doctrine of the Fall, would be consistent with any understanding of the Fall which did not preclude God's activity outside the framework of Christian tradition.

[12] See above, p. 122.

[13] Religious *actions* (including such phenomena as ritual cannibalism) obviously pose special problems which must be considered later. At this point in the discussion, we are concerned with religious worship and the communication of religious meanings.

[14] *The Heretics,* p. 12.

[15] *Ibid.*

[16] Cf. Roland H. Bainton, "The Parable of the Tares as the Proof Text for Religious Liberty to the End of the Sixteenth Century," in *Church History,* I (1932), 3-24.

[17] *On Liberty,* in Edwin A. Burtt (ed.), *The English Philosophers from Bacon to Mill* (New York: Modern Library, 1939 [1859]), pp. 989-90. Cf. Reinhold Niebuhr, *The Nature and Destiny of Man,* pp. 236-37.

[18] *On Liberty,* p. 961.

[19] Several recent theologians have attempted to articulate what could be considered forms of atheism in a theological context. It is too early to offer conclusive assessments of this "death of God" movement, and I have not attempted to relate the movement to the theme of this book. The venture itself seems highly problemati-

cal, particularly if atheism is really intended. Atheism itself seems paradoxical in its relationship to the problem of human freedom. In the most immediate sense, man's freedom and creativity seem enlarged through the loss of transcendent responsibility. Atheism can be proclaimed as a "gospel"; the good news being man's new-found freedom from the tyranny of his inherited conceptions of God. But in a deeper sense, freedom and creativity are empty terms when robbed of ultimate meaning; they become the symbols of tragedy rather than the basis of joy. Moreover, with the loss of transcendent responsibility, the basis is laid for tribal gods and human tyrannies. Finally, to relate this to the problem of chapter III, atheism generally involves absolute claims concerning the nature of reality which could scarcely survive the Protestant critique of absolutes. It attempts in its way to dismiss the infinite and mysterious from the center of being. Regardless, however, of the degree to which these comments are specifically germane to the "death of God" theologians, it is quite conceivable that this theological movement may at least perform the indirect service of helping other Christians to purify their ideas of God. This possibility was quite overlooked by those Christian leaders, including a number of Methodist bishops, who prematurely moved to condemn the movement out of hand. It would be less than charitable to suggest that any of these leaders would contemplate repressive measures, but under different circumstances of time and place religious leaders have often so acted on the basis of premature judgments.

[20] Cf., e.g., H. Richard Niebuhr, *The Social Sources of Denominationalism* (New York: Holt, 1929).

[21] Thus, the most helpful books on right-wing extremism in recent American life have been those which moved beyond mere exposure and moralistic censure to careful interpretation. A good illustration of the possibilities for such interpretation is provided by Daniel Bell (ed.), *The Radical Right* (Garden City, N.Y.: Doubleday, Anchor ed., 1964).

[22] John Courtney Murray, *We Hold These Truths*, p. 14.

V

The Responsible State in Protestant Perspective

Religious liberty is distinctively a political problem, however much it depends upon theological insight for principled solution. Political theory and the social sciences have important contributions to make to our understanding of how theological insight can best be applied to the social and political context. The title of this chapter is not intended to suggest that Protestant Christians necessarily have a theory of the state which is peculiarly their own. Rather, it raises the question how we should view the responsible state in the light of what has previously been said here about Protestant faith. It should be said, however, that Protestant theological insight does have a deep internal relationship with the idea of the responsible state, as it will be developed here. While other religious views may also support this idea, Protestant thought points logically in its direction. Indeed, movements based on Protestant thought have made profound contributions to the development of the responsible state during the centuries which Tillich has called the Protestant Era. Most recently social-political thought within Protestantism and Eastern Orthodoxy (especially in the World Council of Churches) has given powerful new insight through the concept of the "responsible society," a concept which has commended itself to friends of democratic government everywhere, regardless of their religious persuasion.

1. The State and the Idea of Sovereignty

The state has been defined above as society acting as a whole, with the ability to compel. This definition must now be explained more fully and related to the problem of sovereignty.

When we say that the state is society acting as a whole, we are not picturing all the persons in a given society as participating harmoniously in the same activity at the same time. Nor are we saying that the state represents unanimous social agreement upon an action or policy. Total involvement and unanimous agreement are scarcely imaginable in a primitive, much less in a modern, society. Furthermore, even the will of the majority of the people may be frustrated by governors and governments which are supposed to represent the state in actual operation. An adequate definition of the state must therefore have equal applicability to the primitive tribe, the Athens of Socrates, the France of Louis XIV, the China of Mao Tze Tung, and the Western democracies in the contemporary world. How is it that all such "states" may be understood as "society

149

acting as a whole, with the ability to compel"? There are two principal ways.

In the first place, every action of state presupposes the support of the power systems of the entire society. It reflects the monopoly of coercive power. It has no rival within society, for any rival power must be understood as another state. The eminent American sociologist Talcott Parsons has observed that political power is different from other forms of power (such as economic power) in that it is hierarchically structured. Economic power, for instance, is quantitative; which is to say, it is "simply a matter of more or less." Political power, however, is a matter of "higher and lower levels." "The greater power is power *over* the lesser, not merely *more* power *than* the lesser." Political power, therefore, represents "a *mobilization of the total relational* context as a facility relative to the goal in question." [1] Political power "is capacity to control the relational system as a system, whether it be an organization or a diffuse, less integrated system." [2] This understanding of political power is also largely reflected in the views of Professor MacIver, to which reference was made in the second chapter. Although MacIver is reluctant to picture political power in an all-embracing sense (on the ground that "the power wielded by government constitutes only one of several foci and kinds of power within a society" [3]), he goes on to say that political power "alone is the organ of the whole community." As such it requires and demands the "obedience of all who live within its territory." [4] Or, as he has put it in another work,

The state is distinguished from all other associations by its exclusive investment with the final power of coercion. Consequently, its law differs from all other social laws in two ways: first, that there is attached to it the peculiar sanction of socialized and unconditional compulsion; second—a corollary from the first—that it applies without exception to everyone within a geographical area.[5]

If I understand Professors MacIver and Parsons rightly, both find political power in the integration of the power resources of the entire society, although MacIver would be especially careful to say that most of the power resources of society are not political in origin. The meaning of this is that persons and groups within society support the political actions of society whether they like it or not. Therefore, when the state acts, they are also acting— whether they like it or not. I may be opposed to governmental expenditures for military armaments or to the support of this or that war, but my taxes are collected and used for such purposes anyway. That is to say, my power is being used as a part of the power of the whole, even when I do not happen to agree with the ends which it is made to serve. And just as my economic power may be utilized in such a way, even my person may be directly employed by the state to serve ends with which I am not in agreement. The military draft is an obvious illustration. No less real is the fact that all my conduct can be both positively and negatively regulated through law: which is to say that my ability to act with respect to ends is directed. If I choose to resist political power, to refuse to pay taxes, to disobey law—this may indeed mean that my powers will not be used by the state. But the state, then, may destroy the effect of my powers. Even though it may be in a sense weakened thereby, the totality of its control is thereby also illustrated. To concur in this analysis, it is not necessary to say that all power is political in character or in origin. It is merely necessary to agree that all social power is available to the state and is at least implicitly exercised when the state acts as the state—that is, when society acts as a whole.

This points to the second sense in which society acts as a whole. As most political theorists have observed, no state could long outlast the absence of any popular support. Political power which is not considered to be a legitimate exercise of authority by the people of the society will not long be sustained. This is true even under despotism. A despot whose exercise of power over a society is not supported by the consent of the people will have no end of difficulty. Traditionally, political theory has distinguished between power and authority. Power represents the actual capacity to achieve desired ends.[6] Authority reflects social approval of the manner in which that power is exercised (authority may in this sense be described as *legitimate* power). The dependency of the state upon popular consent was understood even by ancient Stoic political theorists, whose thought is so important as a source of modern democratic political developments. The Stoic thinkers invented the fiction that the Roman emperors governed as representatives of the people. The people were thus considered to be the real source of political sovereignty. It is proper to refer to this as a "fiction," since the Roman emperors were hardly responsible to the people in any democratic sense of the word. But there is a deeper sense in which the emperors did represent the people. The people at least considered the imperial rule to be morally binding upon them. In any state the actions of the governor may be said to represent "society acting as a whole" in that there is implied consent to his official actions as a legitimate exercise of political power—again, whether or not there is universal approval of the action as an action. In the absence of political authority (that is, in the absence of consent to the legitimacy of the state) one may truly say that the power exercised is not genuinely political power. It is not the state but some alien power.

This understanding of the nature of the state suggests new appreciation for the general tendency of political contract theories, although the contract theories of Hobbes, Locke, and Rousseau are misunderstood if metaphorical elements are taken literally. When Hobbes speaks of political power as a power which has been accepted by all in an effort to secure universal protection against the disruptive elements in society (man's strong tendencies toward self-centeredness and meanness in relation to his fellows) he has expressed a true understanding of part of the meaning of the state, although he links it with an unacceptably pessimistic understanding of man. When Locke depicts the state as a compact between equal citizens entered into freely and positively, he also expresses a truth concerning the state, even though he seems to suggest mistakenly that individuals consciously enter into such social compacts and that individuals conceivably could exist apart from human society. When Rousseau speaks of the "General Will" he points toward the reality of society acting as a whole and toward the fact that man does, as a social being, find his meaning and fulfillment through society—even though he also conveys the mistaken notion that the "General Will" has concrete existence as such, and even though subsequent political experiments which have drawn inspiration from the idea of "General Will" often have meant the imposition of the will of the few upon that of the many. Such qualifications aside, the whole tendency of contract theory in Western political thought has been to emphasize two truths about the state: first, that the state does represent the whole of society; second, that individual citizens of society participate in the state through their various powers and through their consent to the legitimacy (if not the wisdom) of the actions of the state.

Several additional comments may help prevent misunderstanding.

First, no effort has been made here to identify the state with society as if the terms were simply interchangeable. Nor has the state been identified with government. The state is conceived abstractly as a *function* of society. It is present whenever society is acting as a whole. It is not present in most of the social activities of the persons who make up the society—not even in the totalitarian state, although that kind of state unquestionably intrudes coercive power and the fear of coercive power into a vast range of social life. To conceive of the state as a function of society could be illustrated by comparing it with one's lap. It is the shape of one's body, but one has it only when he is sitting down. It is not present when he is lying down, standing up, walking, or running—just as the state is not present in most of the activities of society, but only when society is in some sense acting as a whole with the ability to compel assent. Government, on the other hand, is understood as the implementation of the state. When society acts as a whole it generally finds certain specialized institutions useful. It may require legislative organs to establish the laws, administrative organs to execute the laws, and judicial institutions to settle disputes concerning the right application of the laws. In modern civilizations, of course, these functions require vast bureaucracies if they are to be properly conducted.

Next, we must recognize that the term "society" is ambiguous when applied to the modern world. What is "a society"? If one understands by the term an association of persons with common institutions and a common culture, there is a sense in which modern life reflects an overlapping and intermingling of societies. It is even possible to discern the emergence of a world community or society—

as evidenced by the rapid growth of common culture and the emergence of universal institutions. To speak of "state" in this context, as we have defined the term, is to suggest that there is in fact no perfect state. No present society possesses entirely the possibility of acting as a whole, although the tendency of society to achieve integration and the capacity to act as a whole is possibly universal. Just as our time is witnessing the emergence of world community, it may be that the most significant political tendency of the present period in history is the gradual replacement of the nation-state system with a world-state one. Since national boundaries to a lesser and lesser degree represent the realities of human community, and since the world itself is conceivable to a greater and greater degree as one society, political institutions and actions must increasingly be universal in dimension.

Furthermore, the morality of political actions is not established simply by their being acts of society as a whole. It is one thing to say that the state does, in some sense, exist by virtue of the people's acceptance of its legitimacy. It is quite another to imply that what the community (or its political leadership) establishes is therefore right or just, that there is no more transcendent frame of reference to judge the rightness of the community than the community itself. The various forms of positivism which have tended toward this conclusion have risked the confusion of the normative realm or value center with the manner of social expression of values or norms. The genius of a responsible state, as we shall see, is that it seeks to provide for the translation of the transcendent values or norms of its citizens into concrete political policy. But reality is more than any society or state, and normative thought derives from perceptions of reality itself, not from society or state alone. This correlates directly with what has been said in previous chapters from a theological viewpoint.[7]

Finally, let us look at the concept of sovereignty. The term, as generally understood, refers to supreme, self-sufficient political power. To speak of a sovereign state is to suggest that the state is the point at which ultimate political power is located—that is, political power which is not formally responsible to some higher power. Political criticism has quite properly rejected pretensions to sovereignty by some part of society over against other parts of society. Even ancient Stoic theory located sovereignty in all the people, thus giving the notion of "popular sovereignty" roots which are much more ancient than most modern democrats suppose. Neither emperor, nor king, nor governor is sovereign. However absolute the appearance of their power, it is still formally responsible to the society which it reflects and integrates. The government, as a set of institutions, is not sovereign for it also is responsible to society. Moreover, in the modern world there is much confusion in speaking of this or that "sovereign nation," for scarcely any nation-state exists which is not to some degree responsible in the exercise of its powers to a wider context. (One can speak of partial sovereignty, of course, in a relative sense. Thus, the United States and the Soviet Union might be considered to be *more* sovereign than, say, the Dominican Republic or Hungary.)

But apart from such qualifications, can even society or "the people" properly be spoken of as sovereign? Jacques Maritain, among some other political theorists, has preferred to say no. Maritain holds that even "the people" lack one indispensable ingredient of sovereignty, which is absolute or transcendent supremacy. "It would," he writes, "be simply non-sensical to conceive of the people governing themselves *separately from themselves and from above*

themselves." [8] On the basis of this observation, he prefers
to discard the concept of sovereignty altogether. But the
context in which he uses the term, and the concerns which
activate his discussion, suggest that Maritain is primarily
interested in undermining the basis in political theory
for totalitarianism. He argues, in effect, that all political
structures, even those which represent the people most
perfectly, must still confront a transcendent frame of reference to which they are responsible. I agree with this concern, as the next section will make clear. But I still consider the term "sovereignty" useful in designating which
human political powers are ultimate or supreme—even
though "sovereignty" finally points in a theological direction which transcends everything human. Political
sovereignty, as a concept, helps us to understand that the
final human source of political power is the people themselves; it is not any prince or president or parliament, nor
any specific institution of government. Only when one locates the place of human sovereignty is it possible to indicate that sovereignty which is above and to which the
human sovereigns are ultimately responsible.

2. The Responsible State

The foregoing discussion does not settle in itself the proper form which the state should assume, although such an
analysis of political power and sovereignty certainly calls
into question any system of government which is imposed
upon people irrespective of their wishes and participation.
If the state represents society acting as a whole, and if
government is therefore *formally* responsible to all the
people, why should it not also be *explicitly* responsible to
all the people? Modern political theory, from the time of
Locke (and excepting only a few nightmarish lapses into
absolutism) has generally been concerned about the peo-

ple's right to govern themselves. Political theory has thus tended to justify self-government—the state organized so as to be explicitly responsible to all the people who comprise society. It could be said that such a state reflects society *consciously* acting as a whole.

The idea of a responsible state is given profound theoretical support by Protestant-Eastern Orthodox ecumenical thought in the conception of the "responsible society." This conception was formulated by the first Assembly of the World Council of Churches which met at Amsterdam in 1948. It has been utilized by subsequent World Council assemblies at Evanston (in 1954) and New Delhi (in 1961) to express ecumenical insight on social questions. The conception is formulated in this way:

A responsible society is one where freedom is the freedom of men who acknowledge responsibility to justice and public order, and where those who hold political authority or economic power are responsible for its exercise to God and the people whose welfare is affected by it.[9]

Political application of this idea is made more concrete in the commentary which followed:

Man must never be made a mere means for political or economic ends. Man is not made for the State but the State for man. . . . For a society to be responsible under modern conditions it is required that the people have freedom to control, to criticize and to change their governments, that power be made responsible by law and tradition, and be distributed as widely as possible through the whole community.[10]

This formula clearly delineates the conception of a responsible political order. It includes within its purview the idea of freedom as the necessary condition of responsibility and the corollary commitment to respect for personality. It includes appreciation for the necessity of order (as opposed to anarchy) and an understanding of justice as the proper end to be sought by the people acting through the instrumentalities of law and government. It contains, moreover, the distinctively theological understanding that all social activity exists in the context of responsibility to God.

The idea of the responsible society, as formulated and applied by the World Council of Churches, is a logical application of the Protestant criticism of idolatry and the Protestant expectancy as discussed in the preceding chapters. Negatively, it resists any absolutizing of a relative political power. Negatively, it will not permit one to presume too much concerning the "divine right" of any human agency of government. In the same sense it would reject the idolatry represented by "divine right of kings" or the "peoples' democratic republic" or the superman of Fascist adulation. Positively, it affirms the capacity of the people for self-government, by which it intends to include all the people. It catches the same meaning as Lincoln's famous epigrams: "no man is good enough to govern another without that other's consent," and "government of the people, by the people, and for the people." Both negatively and positively it reflects the same insight as Reinhold Niebuhr's saying, "Man's capacity for justice makes democracy possible; but man's inclination to injustice makes democracy necessary." [11] A responsible state is one which affords protection against sin and pretension in the guise of government at the same time that it gives opportunity to all the people to assume responsibility for their own political life.

The growth of totalitarianism as a phenomenon in modern civilization has led many thinkers to argue for the limitation of the state as the best way to protect the people from such demonic despotism. Often this is exhibited in a deep fear of government—a fear which has, in our time, fed numerous reactionary political movements which have sought to limit government for the sake of "freedom." Among theologians we have already referred to Emil Brunner and various Roman Catholic thinkers who have also sought to limit the state theoretically as a check against totalitarian excesses of the unlimited state.

It needs to be said here, however, that the problem of freedom is by no means simply one of limiting the power of the state. Indeed, in many cases it is the power of the state which undergirds freedom. Blind fear of the state may result in political policies which undermine freedom more than they protect it. Dean Walter G. Muelder persuasively points to this danger:

Too much thinking about the state today is rooted in fear— fear of power and fear of the historical fact of the totalitarian states. This judgment does not mean that the fear is not related to reality, but a generalized fear reinforces certain tendencies toward misanthropy. Fear of power may increase the power of fear. An overemphasis on the idea of power and the negative function of the state in using physical force inhibits creative thought on how the state, conceived as a limited but responsible association, can be constructively developed as a servant of justice and freedom, perhaps even of love.[12]

Karl Mannheim argues similarly that the state is the very thing which can protect freedom for modern man and that it must be given sufficient power to do so. The following expression is characteristic of his view:

Once we free ourselves of the bogey that whatever the state and its bureaucracy do is wrong and contrary to freedom, and whatever others do is efficient and synonymous with freedom, we can squarely face the true issue. Reduced to a single phrase, the issue is that in our modern world everything is political, the state is everywhere, and public responsibility is interwoven in the whole fabric of society. Freedom consists not in denying this interpenetration but in defining its legitimate uses in all spheres, setting limits and deciding the pattern of penetration and, last but not least, in safeguarding public responsibility and shared control over decisions. From this follows the importance of institutional control for a strategy of reform in a democratically planned society, and the need for a theory of power based on democratic principles.[13]

Obviously, such things are easier to say than to implement in policy—as both Muelder and Mannheim would agree. But such an affirmative view of the state correlates well with the notion of responsibility. The responsible state is explicitly responsible to all the people; it reflects society explicitly acting as a whole. There is no reason why society, acting as a whole, may not seek to create social conditions for its own life which safeguard freedom and which correlate freedom with order and justice.

This suggests another dimension to the word "responsibility." In speaking of a "responsible state" we have been suggesting primarily that the state (in its disposition of power) ought to be responsible *to* all its citizens. The concept of responsibility admits the additional meaning, however, that in the responsible state people can assume responsibility (through the state) *for* their corporate destiny. Insofar as events depend upon human agency, responsibility for their direction is finally human. Moral life consists partly in the recognition that man may affect end results by his activities and the choices he makes. If it is understood that a vast range of results may be attained or obstructed by society acting as a whole, it becomes clear that the state has enormous moral significance as a channel for the moral decision and action of its citizens. I do not mean by this that *all* moral decision and action should or even can be channeled through the state —a pretension which attaches to some extent to Hegelian and post-Hegelian theories. But certainly the state is the arena for *much* moral action and decision. Indeed, proper moral action and decision by the state is important because it is needed to safeguard the possibilities of other, nonpolitical, areas for ethical action and decision. This result must often be attained through the deliberate self-limitation of the state. In American history and tradition, the creation of constitutional government was largely a deliberate act to limit the range of political action so that areas for free, private action would be safeguarded. Such self-limitation does not hinge upon the mistaken notion that the state does not have the *power* to affect this or that social structure, but rather that it *chooses not to do so*. In our day, the fulfillment of the moral possibilities in political life requires a much deeper awareness of just how much the state *can* do so that there can be more deliberate, moral choice of what the state *should* and *will* do. The basic objective of the state will be defined by moral consensus as to the ideal society. And this objective will include all the conditions considered necessary for man's social fulfillment in community.

Before proceeding, I want to point out that while much of this may seem similar to Marxist thought, it in fact represents sharp divergence from Marxism. In classical Marxist theory one encounters the view that real, authentic human history will only begin at that (future) time when society is able to assume full responsibility for its own direction: i.e., at the point when exploitation and class struggle cease to alienate man from society and thus to deprive society of its creative freedom. But the present analysis by no means accepts or depends upon the view that "class struggle" is the sole impediment to the achievement of the responsible society. Moreover, Marxism itself has been singularly naïve in its rejection of the state as a permanently necessary function of human society, the focal point of social regulation, coercion, and common action in the interests of justice. In practice, of course, Marxist Communism has often presented ruling oligarchies with vast opportunities to rule irresponsibly. Since, in a democratic society, economic power is formally subservient to political power, there is thus a curious sense in which the people in one of the Western democracies may actually have more power over the course of economic life than they do in the Communist lands! But to participate in the full moral meaning of responsibility persons in all societies must recognize that the state can do almost anything in their behalf. And negatively all must realize that their power today even extends to the possibility of the suicide of mankind through nuclear war. Marxism has enough of a commitment to social responsibility built into its theoretical foundations to open up wide possibilities for further development in the direction of responsibility. Clearly it is the responsibility of Christians in dialogue with Marxists to encourage such tendencies.

The full meaning of the responsible state, then, is unfolded in political institutions which make it possible for the widest number of people to participate in political decision, with the fullest possible understanding of the disposable power available to society acting as a whole. It is implicit that every person who thus participates in the political life of community does so on the basis of normative understandings and loyalties which transcend the political community itself. Man was not made for the state, but the state for man.

3. Consensus and Majority Rule

It is easy enough to speak of the "responsible state" in the abstract; but it is quite another thing to work this ideal out in the actual government of a society. Just as Rousseau's idea of the "general will" was only grotesquely reflected in the revolutionary French government, so "responsible state" finds frustration in even the most democratic society. How can "the people" arrive at consensus? How is the consensus related to real action by the state? How is dissent related to consensus? How is the possibility of dissent logically preserved by the actions of "society acting responsibly as a whole"?

The idea of responsible state could not imply that the state must await unanimity before it could act—in the manner of Quaker fellowship. Some formula must define the point at which action may proceed in the absence of total unanimity. Historically, democratic societies have often been based upon majority rule. The idea of majority rule may be understood as a logical consequence of the responsible state, because the latter assumes the equality of all its citizens. Responsible state implies the equality of its citizens; not in the sense of their equality of endowment, etc., but in the sense of their human equality (none may be presumed to be more human than any other) and their political equality (none may be presumed to be more a citizen than any other). Theologically, Christians view this equality as being rooted in man's common relationship to God as the center of being and value; or, as Richard Niebuhr has put it, "it is by virtue and in respect of their relation to that creative center that they are equal." [14] This equality entails equal concern by the state for the welfare of every man and equal presumption by the state of the potential usefulness of the ideas of every man. Majority rule follows logically from this. If all men are formally equal, then the relative merit of contending positions may be ascertained numerically—so far as the presumption of the state is concerned. The minority may be right on any given issue, of course, but, since it represents fewer people, the position representing the greater number of people must be permitted to govern. A responsible state may, with consistency, make constitutional provision to guard against a temporary and small majority using its power to destroy the very basis of responsible government or otherwise infringing upon the possibility of the minority's participation in the ongoing political process. Such provision may take the form of more complex processes of decision-making and review, and it may include the requirement that the more serious issues should be determined by larger majorities (such as two thirds). The latter would simply mean that a minority of sufficient size would be able to stop the majority from rushing into a serious action too precipitously.

I have said that the responsible state in the modern world must be free to act upon a wider range of concerns than is generally supposed. Does the concept of the responsible state itself pose limitations upon that range of concerns? Specifically, may the state act with respect to religion? Given the responsible state's responsibility for determining so far as possible its destiny and the conditions of its life, why ought the state to inhibit itself at the point of religious commitment? Is religion a proper object for the consensus of the state? One could make a certain case for formal religious commitment by a whole society, so long as the freedom of minorities to advance their contrary claims were guarded—so that the state's formal commitment could be changed by the same democratic procedures which established it in the first place. Indeed, one could assert that such a procedure is already implicit in principle in the ability of the majority to determine the ultimate directions to be taken by the society, since questions of direction and policy always assume a realm of ultimate valuation.

On the strength of such a view, many friends of religious liberty have argued that the state should acknowledge the basic religious commitment of the majority of its citizens—particularly if that religious commitment is considered an essential support for liberty itself. Furthermore, it is argued by many that some sort of religious commitment is necessary for the sake of social unity, since shared values form the basis of society. Bishop Lesslie Newbigin is typical of many friends of religious liberty who consider that the state must commit itself religiously when he writes as follows:

We are more and more bound to recognize that moral standards depend upon religious or ideological faith. If a government puts down a religious practice like *sutee,* it does so on grounds which are ultimately religious or ideological. Here, therefore, one religious faith confronts another, and one uses the power of government to stop another. It is impossible to evade the perplexity of this problem simply by saying that such things ought not to be done.[15]

Professor Waldo Beach, noting that theories of religious liberty for the past four centuries have tended toward secularism, expresses concern in these words:

The most marked drift is from a religiously based theory of freedom of worship, claiming or allowing a variety of Christian consciences to worship God in whatever way seemed true,

166

to a secular theory of religious freedom, which allows *any* conscience, Christian or atheist, equal protection of the laws. To the liberal this trend may constitute progress, but to the Christian there are serious ambiguities.[16]

The reason why the Christian sees serious moral am-biguities in this trend is partly that "if indeed Christian faith and piety are in some sense necessary to the health of the body politic, then a secular tolerance of indifference which recognizes no greater worth to faith than unfaith may prove to have conceded too much from the cause of truth to the cause of peace, and betrayed true liberty of conscience." [17]

But, aside from the obvious problems which accompany the inclusion of religion as a proper object for political consensus (such as bitter religious antagonism and the difficulties of "establishment" which will be discussed later), it rests upon confusion between policy and the ultimate sources of policy in a responsible state. The very possibility of an "opposition" in the responsible state de-rives from the assumption that all issues ultimately are open issues. Policy must be determined and action must proceed. But the justification of policy and action remains open. A democratic society may—indeed must—agree upon courses of action. But it can never commit itself to the ultimate rightness of given policies of action.

In one sense this rules out the possibility of a "public philosophy" for a democratic society if such a philosophy is detailed with respect to its metaphysical commitments. If, however, "public philosophy" is limited to a theoreti-cal justification of democracy in terms of social pragmatism (in support of certain values of public order) or in terms even of an ultimate statement of the limitations of human understanding, it may be both possible and inescapable.

Indeed, a theory of the nature of man seems in this sense to be implied by democratic society. But such a society can never presume to say why it is that this or that person or group finds it desirable to support it. The interior relationship between responsible state and Protestant theological views as developed in the present volume seems clear enough. On this basis Protestants can understand why they support this kind of state, and non-Protestants can be given assurance that Protestants will not lag in their adherence to the responsible state. But this does not necessarily mean that everybody who supports this kind of state is a Protestant Christian.

"What are we going to do?" is a legitimate political question. But it is not legitimate to inquire, *politically*, "what are we going to believe?" Belief is one-by-one. Nobody can do anybody else's believing or valuing for him. Anybody who asserts that the state can believe anything suffers confusion. Society can act as a whole, but it cannot believe as a whole. Therefore that state lies which proclaims unanimity of belief among its members. In this sense every society is pluralistic—even though there may be broad similarity and commonality among people as to the center of value around which they organize their lives, and even though there may be even greater consensus with respect to other things.

But the most important point to be emphasized here is that unless every question is finally left open, and the conscience of every man fully respected, the notion of responsible state is illusory. The basis of unity of the state is not uniformity of thought or religion, but, rather, it is the dialogue of free men who agree to live together in society. In the actions of such a society policies logically derived from the religious commitments of a majority may often be given the force of law—as when the United States

Supreme Court denied Mormons the right to practice po-
lygamy and when the government of India acted to interfere with *sutee*. But such actions never carry the connota-
tion that the issue is closed or that it may not some day
be reversed by the minority if the minority can manage
to become the majority position.

4. Political Rights in the Responsible State

On the basis of the foregoing, it is clear that in the responsible state political rights are of the profoundest importance. Yet much discussion of rights fails to articulate
precisely their relationship to a total theory of the state.
Moreover, such discussion often rests upon indefensibly
absolute statements about rights. The term "inalienable
rights," however precious in the political rhetoric of
Americans, well illustrates the confusion which is per-
petuated by lack of careful thought about the actual relationship between rights and the state.

Taken literally, it should be obvious that no rights are
"inalienable." One cannot conceive of any claimed rights
which have not at some time or place been totally denied
or "alienated" by the state or even freely surrendered by a
visionless people. Most of the "inalienable rights" for the
American Constitution or the Universal Declaration of
Human Rights of the United Nations are in fact fragile
flowers which require the most careful cultivation,
nourishment, and protection. A further danger in speaking about rights too absolutely is that one may be ill prepared for analysis of conflicts between supposedly absolute rights. An excellent illustration of such conflict and
confusion was afforded by the celebrated "Proposition 14"
campaign in the 1964 elections of the State of California.
At issue was a ballot proposition which, if passed, would
amend the state constitution in such a way that no po-

litical agency of the state could henceforth interfere with the "absolute" right of an owner of property to dispose of that property in any way he should see fit. Actually designed to destroy "fair housing" legislation (legislation to forbid discrimination in the sale or rental of housing), the proposed amendment was justified philosophically as a defense of "property rights." Opponents of the measure based their opposition to it with equal absoluteness on "property rights," but *they* conceived of property rights in terms of the right of every man to have access to property, regardless of his race, creed, or national origin. The campaign was characterized by great bitterness, much of which might have been avoided had the people generally been prepared to discuss the nature of rights in terms of the basis of rights, not merely by asserting dogmatic claims.[18]

What *is* the basis of rights? Political rights may be understood as claims which an individual or group have upon the rest of the community which are protected by the state. A right, therefore, roots in the question of whether a corresponding ethical claim does, in fact, exist between the individual or group and society. Sidney Hook has shown in an illuminating essay on freedom that the question of rights raises the prior question whether the political community ought or ought not enforce this or that claim of the individual in relation to society. The following paragraph summarizes his discussion:

It seems clear that whenever we assert that we have a right, whatever else we are asserting, we are asserting or making a claim. If in fact it is a claim to goods or services which society stands ready to enforce, we call it a legal right. But the question we are concerned with is not what is a legal right, not what claims are actually enforced, but what claims *should* be enforced, what *should* be recognized as basic legal rights for all members of the community. As soon as we grasp this distinction, it is obvious that all questions of basic rights involve claims on other persons and therefore are questions of ethics. A right is a claim which entails an obligation or duty on the part of others in specified times and circumstances to recognize it whether in fact the law does so at the moment.[19]

In establishing and guaranteeing rights, therefore, the state constitutes the manner of its own life in harmony with the ethical perceptions of those who control its disposable power. In the case of the responsible state, political rights reflect the ethical perceptions of the majority of the people.

Here again we can see both truth and error in a more positivistic view of rights. Rights are indeed designated and protected by the state, but the state is not the *source* of rights. The source is to be found in the ethical perceptions of the people. It raises questions about the centers of value of the people—questions which the state, as such, cannot answer. Certain rights are of course well-nigh universal and point to ethical perceptions which are inclusive of most human religious differences. For example, almost all (if not all) societies prohibit murder and protect property in some manner. The near universality of such rights (to life and property), however divergent in form, gives rise to ethical discussion of natural law which can be perceived irrespective of religious faith. The very notion of a responsible state rests upon ethical perceptions which are broader than any particular religious faith, although it may be given specific justification by particular faith commitments—as I believe it is by Protestant Christianity.

Rights also need to be understood in two different senses. There are some rights which afford protection of the individual or group from the activity of the state. Such rights represent the self-restraint of the state—or the commitment of the majority (or those who hold the power of the state) not to exercise that power with respect to the minority in specified ways. Religious liberty, for example, partly indicates the commitment of the state not to coerce the religious expressions of its citizens. But rights may also represent the active intervention of the state to prevent individual groups or citizens from infringing upon one another's lives in specified ways. The state protects citizens' lives from murder by other citizens, it protects their property from theft, etc. (Fair housing legislation establishes and protects the right of acquisition of property against discriminatory actions by other citizens.) Religious liberty may also be a right of this sort—as a protection by the state of the right of persons not to be molested by other persons in the free exercise of their religious faith. Both kinds of rights are important. But the distinction is also important, particularly since those who fear government are likely to overlook the protective role of government and to weaken that role while seeking protection *from* government.

A responsible state will, by definition, be concerned about one formal right: the right of all members of the society to participate in political life. This right must include the right to participate in political decision-making, the right of access to all sources of information (as Alexander Meiklejohn has put it, the people, "as rulers . . . cannot govern wisely unless they have complete access to both fact and opinion" [20]), and the right to freedom of expression. Religious liberty inheres in each of these rights: in political participation, as obedience to religious dictates; in the right of access to all sources of information, so that religious obedience can be intelligently implemented and so that no channel of access to reality will be closed by an alien power; and in the right of expression, so that one can bear witness to one's values and seek to convert others to them. These matters will be considered more fully in the next chapter. The structure of rights and freedoms of a responsible state have been summarized excellently by John Stuart Mill in his essay *On Liberty,* and before him by John Milton in his classic *Areopagitica.*

A Christian will be concerned about an added dimension of rights which is really implied in the concept of responsible state, but not so obviously. That is the right of every man to the conditions necessary for participation in the life of community. I have in mind something more than the political rights of freedom of speech, access to information, etc. The Christian understanding of justice is deeper. It holds it to be the moral claim of every person to be accepted as a person by the rest of society. While the state clearly cannot require persons to love one another, it clearly *can* regulate conditions so that all persons at least have access to community in the fullest sense. Much of the contemporary American Civil Rights Movement is concerned in this way with equal access to the conditions of communal living: jobs, housing, public accommodations, social welfare protection for the jobless or persons in special economic need, education, and contact through educational institutions with the broad diversity of the community. Under modern urban and industrial conditions law must take cognizance of new impediments to the full expression of life in community and must deal with them. Such rights are also related to the idea of a responsible state, because political participation is largely fictional for those who are denied the broader right to participate as persons in society.

Political rights are thus rooted in ethical concern and

are variable with the conditions facing a given society. Formally, however, such rights must guard the ability of all persons to participate in the life of the community if the state is to merit the adjective "responsible."

5. A Note on the Efficiency of the Responsible State

Arguments for the responsible state, with its assumed structure of rights and duties, are basically ethical rather than pragmatic. In an earlier chapter we took note that the question of the health or viability of a society is not finally a decisive argument for religious liberty—even though it is a powerful support for religious liberty to be able to argue that it brings such social benefits in its wake.

It is worth remembering here, however, that the responsible state and religious liberty ultimately *are* more efficient, or at least healthier, than closed societies in which religious conformity is required and freedom of expression circumscribed. It is rightly understood that the responsible state reflects the only society in which social integration and public order are not threatened by legitimate discontent. In every state where power is controlled by selfish minorities, where power may not be challenged openly by those who have been treated unjustly, an unresolved tension exists. Where people are not free to change their governments in an orderly and responsible way, they may be strongly tempted to do so by revolution and bloodshed. This may be expressed theologically by saying that God guarantees the impermanence of the unjust order.[21] The irresponsible state harbors enemies within itself.

Against this view it may, of course, be argued that many authoritarian regimes have been perfectly stable because they were accepted even by people who had no voice in them. If every citizen believes in the divine right of king or emperor, then king or emperor will be obeyed more or

174

less willingly whether or not most people agree with specific laws or policies. In the modern world, however, such absolutism has lost its legitimation, and even in preceding eras the record of irresponsible monarchy is not very good in terms of social stability. It is even worse when one considers the health, rather than simply the stability, of society. As MacIver has reminded us, the kind of spontaneity which is necessary if a culture is to be vital and creative cannot flower under politically repressive conditions. It is appalling to think of the great waste of creative human resources which has resulted from despotism. Where the surface is calm with no seething currents in the depths waiting to burst forth, the water is apt to be quite stale. Mussolini may have been able to make the trains run on time, but that is poor consolation for the reduction of society to mere mechanical obedience to command.

Similar comments may be made about societies which attempt to use religion for the purpose of social integration, despite the fact that the religion is not actually shared by everybody. The social integration thus achieved is bound to be contrived. It will lessen the vitality of the integrating religion even among its own adherents. Idolatrous religion of this sort probably impedes genuine social integration, because it destroys the personal freedom without which integration is merely mechanical. This does not mean that shared religious meanings may not best serve the function of social integration. Surely shared religious meanings are the best possible source of social integration. But they must be in fact genuinely shared, and they must not remain idolatrously closed to ever new dimensions of meaning.

The responsible state is bound, at times, to appear unstable and disorderly, because it allows full rein to the ferment of disagreement and dialogue. But such conflict can be healthy if those who participate in it also acknowledge responsibility to public order and the rights of others.

6. The Responsible State and the Sovereign God

How, then, must the responsible state be understood in Protestant theological perspective? I believe one can make no less a claim than to say that it is the state which offers the most possibilities for God's actual rule in human society. The responsible state is not formally derived from theological reflection. It is not a theocratic political order in any traditional sense of the term. Many, perhaps most, of those who are committed to the responsible state in the modern world are not Christians, much less Protestant Christians. Non-Christians may well see the responsible state as politically essential if they are to live lives of freedom and creativity, with equal opportunity to give effect to their values through the political order.

Nevertheless, in Protestant perspective we may understand that such a state best makes it possible for God to speak his word through all men, so that history may be directed toward divine purposes. A responsible state may be expected to make mistakes. It will succumb to this or that idolatry. The perceptions of its citizens will be human, not divine. All the same, so long as openness prevails, mistakes can convey their own lessons regarding truth, and they can be corrected. Faith in this process does not require excessive optimism. If it did, the whole human political enterprise would be a doubtful business.

In this perspective the ecumenical idea of responsible society, including as it does the acknowledgment of "responsibility to God," attains broad foundation. It is most appropriately fulfilled where men consciously acknowledge their responsibility to God. But the phrase can include all those who acknowledge responsibility to a center of value which is beyond themselves and also beyond idolatry. One must recall here Tillich's insight that the Protestant understanding of justification by faith applies even to the person who is honestly in the situation of doubt. Serious doubt pays tribute to the seriousness of truth. Therefore, even those who do not find it possible to pay conscious tribute to God as revealed in Christ and Christian tradition can serve as a political channel for the sovereignty of God if they take value and reality seriously. The responsible state is the state in which persons are most encouraged to implement their dearest values politically and where they are least impeded from doing so.

I want to anticipate some later discussion at this point with a comment regarding current Protestant positions on matters of church-state relations. In his study of *Protestant Concepts of Church and State,* Sanders distinguishes between the "Separationists" and the "Transformationists." The former are held to be oriented basically toward the separation of church and state; the latter toward the religious transformation of public life. In the perspective of this and the preceding chapters, it may be theologically necessary to combine the true insights of each of these orientations despite the fact that, as actual movements in contemporary Protestant thought, they often appear contradictory. The true tendency of the separationist is to spare the state from making religious commitments for all the people (whether they agree with them or not) and to protect the whole range of religious liberties even of those who appear committed to no religion or at least to no culturally recognized religion. In this tendency, the separationist clearly reflects both the Protestant critique of idolatry and the Protestant expectancy. It also reflects the high tradition of the responsible state—for it takes seriously the state's equal obligation to all its citizens, not just those who accept a received religious tradition. This tendency, therefore, is one which must be included in some form in any adequate Protestant approach to religious liberty and church-state relations. The tendency of the transformationist, on the other hand, is to seek to shape society and the public order in obedience to the will of God. In this, the transformationist obviously takes seriously the transcendent sovereignty of God and knows that to discover his will is the chief interest of every Christian and to obey his will is his chief occupation. This also reflects the high tradition of the responsible state, for the responsible state depends utterly upon the full political participation of persons who earnestly and selflessly grapple with serious issues and who seek the highest public good. In this sense, de Tocqueville was absolutely right in his observation that the less coercive and dictatorial the political institutions of society, the more they depend upon religious commitments to restrain rulers and ruled and to shape the direction of their political involvements.[22] But separationism and transformationism are by no means inconsistent. Protestant separationism is miserably applied by those who argue that the church has no business concerning itself with political analysis and judgment (an argument which regularly appears whenever the direction of that analysis and judgment contradicts the special interests of those whose concerns may be less over the inner intention of separation of church and state than they are over their special privileges). Protestant transformationism is also poorly applied by those who think of transformation in terms of using public power for the manipulation of religious symbols and the imposition of religious traditions (at grave risk of idolatry) upon those whose religious perceptions are different.

Christians best serve the sovereign God where they seek to apply his will as they understand it, but where they also take seriously the possibility that God will speak through others in different, not anticipated ways. The responsible state is the one in which this can best proceed.

NOTES

[1] Talcott Parsons, *The Social System* (Glencoe, Ill.: The Free Press, 1951), p. 126.

[2] *Ibid.*

[3] *The Web of Government*, p. 87.

[4] *Ibid.*, p. 94.

[5] Robert M. MacIver and Charles H. Page, *Society: An Introductory Analysis* (New York: Rinehart and Co., 1949), p. 456.

[6] Careful consideration of the term "power" requires certain refinements. As I have been using it here, it must be understood as political power, or nonpoliticial power which is translatable *into* political power. Some forms of power probably resist or defy such translation. But the following examples may illustrate how nonpolitical power can be translated into political power: (1) Powers of economic productivity translate readily into taxes, and thence into such public facilities as schools, highways, government buildings, and military supplies. (2) The power of prestige may be manipulated to serve political ends, as when famous persons lend their prestige to political campaigns or when prestige symbols are used in propaganda. (3) Even spiritual power, or charisma, may be important to sway multitudes of people, thus gaining popular support for political programs or candidates. In analyzing power precisely it is important to ask what, exactly, a specified power can achieve and how that power can be made to have indirect political effects.

[7] There is an excellent discussion of this problem in Muelder, *Foundations of the Responsible Society*, pp. 105-6. He writes that "one of the crying needs of the nation is for a return to the understanding of the moral and social foundations of law and politics, the strengthening of its roots by moral renewal in all social groups from the family to the state, and a rebirth of the sense of the vocation of

politics as a sacred religious and moral duty on the part of churches and others" (p. 106).

[8] *Man and the State* (Chicago: University of Chicago Press, 1951), pp. 38, 44.

[9] Amsterdam Assembly, *The Church and the Disorder of Society* (1948), p. 192.

[10] *Ibid.*

[11] *The Children of Light and the Children of Darkness* (New York: Scribner's, 1944), p. xi.

[12] *Foundations of the Responsible Society*, p. 108.

[13] *Freedom, Power, and Democratic Planning* (New York: Oxford University Press, 1950), pp. 44-45.

[14] *Radical Monotheism*, p. 73.

[15] Quoted in Carrillo, *The Basis of Religious Liberty*, p. 129.

[16] In Franklin H. Littell (ed.), *Reformation Studies* (Richmond, Va.: John Knox Press, 1962), p. 211.

[17] *Ibid.*

[18] The fact that the measure was adopted by a vote of nearly two to one also illustrates the political mischief which can result from the failure to understand the basis of rights—even though it may be that racial fears and prejudices of the majority had more effect upon their judgment than did their understanding or misunderstanding of the nature of rights.

[19] Sidney Hook, p. 4. *The Paradoxes of Freedom.*

[20] As summarized by Stringfellow Barr, "Censorship in a Dialectical Republic," in John Cogley (ed.), *Religion in America* (New York: Meridian Books, Inc., 1958), p. 210.

[21] The phrase is Walter G. Muelder's.

[22] Quoted by Semour Martin Lipset, "Political Sociology," in R. K. Merton, L. Broom, and L. S. Cottrell, Jr. (eds.), *Sociology Today: Problems and Prospects* (New York: Harper Torchbook ed., 1965 [1959]), I, 88.

VI

From Principle to Policy

This book attempts to locate the most dependable basis for religious liberty in Protestant Christian faith. I have suggested that this basis has both a negative or critical aspect and a positive or constructive one. The *negative* aspect is in the criticism of idolatry: God is always more than any human symbol or institution by which he is represented. The effect of this criticism is to undercut the claim of absoluteness which is implicit in religious intolerance and repression. The *positive* aspect is in the belief in the direct access of any man to the divine. The basis of this affirmation is faith in the sovereignty of God: if God is sovereign, it is blasphemous of any man or state to prejudge absolutely the ways in which he may break into human history. The effect of this affirmation is to create the expectancy that any form of human worship or witness *may* contain something of the divine which is needful to the common life of mankind. Both the negative and the positive aspects of Protestant Christian faith logically sustain the principle of the responsible state, although that concept is not exclusively Protestant or Christian. The idea of responsible state is that the political order should consciously reflect the participation of all its citizens. The corollary of this idea is freedom of expression and access to the conditions necessary for participation in the life of society. Another corollary is the conscious responsibility of the state for the whole life of society—even though the appropriate exercise of that responsibility may often be the constitutional limitation of the powers of government.

In the preceding pages I have occasionally referred to a concrete problem as a means of illustrating the meaning of a principle. In the present chapter I wish to do this more directly. Since the main purpose of the book is to discuss the *basis* of religious liberty, no effort can be made here to settle every problem of policy in a systematic way. Some discussion of the relationship between the principled basis and specific policy may, however, be useful in suggesting how the basis may help to clarify some of the difficult problems which continue to plague us.

1. The Problem of Religious Liberty

That religious liberty is important and that it is required by Christian faith has been said throughout this book. Problems remain, however, concerning religious liberty as applied in actual political policy. I have assumed that the term religious liberty applies not only to that inner religious freedom which may properly be considered both absolute and undeniable, but to the social and political expression of religion as well. The question is whether there are any limits which the state may (or must) properly place upon the latter; and, if so, whether this damages the theoretical basis as discussed above.

In a thoughtful discussion of this problem, Carrillo has pointed out that religious liberty is divisible into different elements. Summarizing ecumenical conversations on this problem, he distinguishes four levels in the expression of religious liberty: (1) Liberty of Conscience, (2) Liberty of Religious Expression, (3) Liberty of Religious Association, and (4) Corporate and Institutional Religious Freedom.[1] His method of establishing the basis and proper limits of each of these levels is interesting. Only the first (Liberty of Conscience) is "pure" religious liberty, to be derived from the theological basis as such. The second, third, and fourth exist as combinations of pure religious liberty and some broader human right. Thus, the liberty of religious expression is based upon religious liberty in combination with the human right of expression and is subject to limitations normal to the latter. Liberty of religious association is based upon religious liberty in combination with the human right of association. And corporate and institutional religious freedom is comprised by religious liberty plus the human right of corporate freedom. This is a useful reminder that when we speak of religious liberty we must understand the different levels of its meaning. As Carrillo has advanced it, the formulation is also a way of guarding the absoluteness of religious freedom ("inasmuch as it protects man's eternal relations with God") but at the same time of providing a basis for those operational limitations which must be accepted as a protection against social abuses. Insofar as religious expression is social it must, in other words, face the same limitations as nonreligious social expressions.

I see little reason for objecting to this approach, although it may obscure several issues which need to be clarified further. First, it may obscure the fact that in some cases religious expression needs to be privileged beyond the point of the broader human right to which it corresponds. This would not be so obvious when we speak of the human right of expression, for it is close to being absolute in and of itself in a responsible society. But for human right of corporate freedom the case may not be so clear. A religious institution, serving explicitly religious ends, would seem to have rights of existence and expression which are more absolute than, for instance, economic institutions such as business corporations. Whereas the latter may be limited by the state, perhaps even legislated out of existence in the interest of social justice, it is difficult to conceive of the responsible state similarly limiting the religious institution insofar as it serves distinctively religious ends. I am not suggesting that a religious institution should be absolutely privileged, particularly since most religious institutions also serve nonreligious ends. But it is very doubtful whether one can simply equate the case for corporate and institutional religious freedom with the case for the human right of corporate freedom. Similar points could be made about the liberty of association, although the human right of association is itself doubtless much broader than the human right of corporate freedom (as Carrillo has distinguished between the two).

Another point which his formulation may obscure is the fact that the ultimate justification of most human rights as such may be religious, based on religious presuppositions. This would be the claim of those who say that religious liberty is the most fundamental human right. The reason is not difficult to establish. Religion is man's ultimate concern. Religion is the source of the values and purposes which ultimately give direction to all human enterprise. When one speaks of human rights, those rights would in an important sense be meaningless were there no implied religious dimension in life. To make religious liberty dependent for its application upon a human right partly obscures the reciprocal dependence of that human right upon religious liberty. By entering such qualifications I do not wish to obscure the contribution which Carrillo has made with this formulation, for it would certainly not endanger religious liberty in any state where Protestant criticism and expectancy were accepted as the appropriate basis for that liberty.

In an effort at further clarification, however, I would like to suggest three distinguishable categories of religious freedom. Underlying all three categories is the assumption that the state presumes the religious beliefs of all its citizens to be respected and taken seriously—even though conflicting religious beliefs within the body politic make it impossible for all of them to serve as the basis for political action. The three categories may be termed *absolute, qualified absolute,* and *qualified.*

Absolute religious liberty, corresponding to the pure religious liberty of Carrillo, is the internal freedom to believe and worship as one pleases. No state could conceivably violate this freedom on the basis of the Christian faith, and if it did so for other reasons it would have to be challenged by Christians. One may wonder about the need for even mentioning political interference with internal freedom. There seems to be no way in which the state could interfere with this freedom even if it wished. Yet there is a sense in which the state, were it so minded, could infringe upon absolute religious liberty, namely by requiring its citizens to profess beliefs or values which they do not hold. Absolute religious liberty clearly requires that no person under any circumstances be forced to profess what he does not believe. Absolute religious liberty is at least absolute freedom to maintain silence and internal dissent. Such a freedom has not been maintained universally. It has been abused even in modern times and even in relatively democratic societies. Violations in Fascist or Marxist lands (where "thought control" has a particularly relevant meaning) may readily be identified. It has also been the practice in certain Roman Catholic, Moslem, and Buddhist lands to place heavy legal disabilities upon those refusing to profess the dominant faith. Even in the United States the right of public schools to place children under a certain amount of pressure to join in the recitation of corporate prayer has only recently been questioned. Moreover, legal disabilities have often accompanied the reluctance of persons to sign loyalty oaths or to participate in the recitation of a pledge of allegiance to the flag, even when the reason given for not making this kind of affirmation was that it would conflict with a more ultimate religious loyalty (as in the case of Jehovah's Witnesses). The fact that an affirmation of loyalty to the state may not be a religious question with most people does not make it any less so for those who consider it to be such a question. Compulsion to make verbal affirmations which do not correspond to inner convictions is in conflict with absolute religious liberty and thus may be rejected absolutely as a matter of political policy. If the state exercises such coercion it is presuming the absolute validity of the required affirmation, and it is denying the possibility that the minority may be communicating something of the divine through their dissent. Both presumptions are not possible in the Protestant perspective.

Qualified absolute religious liberty (if such a combination of adjectives be permitted) is the freedom to profess or to express one's faith verbally through social communication. It is the freedom to witness to one's faith, to attempt to gain wider understanding and acceptance of it, to seek to draw others into the worship which it holds central. Why must such freedom be *qualified* at all? Surely the basis of religious liberty as advanced in this book would apply categorically to all efforts to communicate one's faith. It would indeed, because it is assumed that no single religious expression should be absolutized as a final manifestation of the divine and also because the possibility of important truth and value cannot be prejudged in human communication. Furthermore, the religious freedom of expression and the religious obligation to act in the political realm carry with them the need for complete access to sources of opinion and information. (Alexander Meiklejohn observed that, since the people under a democratic constitution are all rulers, they may claim the rightful prerogative of all rulers to complete information.) It is presumptuous of any state bearing or aspiring to the name "responsible" to erect any slight obstacle to complete freedom of expression of religion. This is the absolute aspect of such a freedom.

I am not entirely convinced of the *qualified* aspect myself, although a case must be made for limiting speech which is not designed as communication of faith, knowledge, or opinion but as malicious slander or incitement to action of an illegal sort. The phrase "verbal action" has sometimes been used to designate such incitement because it is taken to be less a form of communication than a form of action. The celebrated illustration is shouting "fire!" in a crowded theater or inflaming a mob to violence. To the extent that such expression must be limited, it partakes of the same limiting qualifications as actions themselves (which will be discussed below). The United States Supreme Court applied this limiting qualification with these words:

187

There are certain well-defined and narrowly limited classes of speech, the prevention and punishment of which has never been thought to raise any Constitutional problem. These include the lewd and obscene, the profane, the libelous, and the insulting or "fighting" words—those which by their very utterance inflict injury or tend to incite an immediate breach of peace. It has well been observed that such utterances are no essential part of any exposition of ideas and are of such slight social value as a step to truth that any benefit that may be derived from them is clearly outweighed by the social interest in order and morality.[2]

There is a certain danger, of course, that so much limitation opens the door to broad interpretations which bite deeply into liberty of religious expression itself. American society in the 1950's provided an illustration. The Communist Party was essentially ruled to be illegal on the grounds of its alleged commitment to the overthrow of the government by force and violence—even despite the renunciation of this Marxian tenet by the party's constitution. Communists were effectively forced underground— out of the dialogue where the possible contributions of Marxism might have been made more readily available and where the weaknesses and fallacies (and dangers) of that system might more readily have been disposed of. Even though Marxism is not a theistic religion, the case provides a good illustration of how what is essentially a religious point of view could be silenced on the ground of its being verbal action rather than legitimate communication—however remote the dangerous effects of such "action" might in fact be.

For the sake of the crowded theater and the lynch mob, one should probably accept the limitation upon "verbal action," but I would insist that this never be applied to the communication of a point of view—particularly one which somebody finds convincing enough to base his whole life upon. Unpopular religious points of view, ranging from Communism to Fascism and racism, will not be improved by being driven underground, and they are probably the ultimately decisive contemporary tests of both Protestant critique and Protestant expectancy.

The problem of religious association and religious institutions, which Carrillo has raised, should principally be located in relation to religious communication. Insofar as such associations and institutions are necessary and desirable for the communication of a religious point of view and for the conduct of worship, their freedom should be virtually absolute. The only limitation here, again, would be insofar as such institutions have broader social effects unrelated to their religious purposes which must be disciplined for the sake of social justice. There is no reason why churches, for instance, should be tax exempt, even if "the power to tax may become the power to destroy." At the same time, the responsible state must not only passively accept the freedom of religious expression; it must actively promote the conditions necessary to its meaningful occurrence. More will be said about this below.

Qualified religious liberty is the freedom to *act* in accordance with one's religious insights and values. The freedom is important and must be safeguarded. It includes the freedom to participate responsibly in the political life of society. It includes overt acts of worship, forms of disciplined ethical observance or abstinences, or acts of charitable public welfare. It is necessary to complete the religious life, and insofar as the state's *presumption* is concerned, it must always be assumed that such action is undertaken with integrity. This form of religious liberty raises problems, however, when it is made into an absolute. For example, what should be done in the case of a small child who obviously needs medical attention (such as a blood transfusion) if its parents, who belong to a sect which has religious objections, refuse to give permission? What should be done where parents refuse to enroll their children in any school on religious grounds, thus saddling the children with insuperable handicaps in their later lives? What should be done with religious groups whose forms of overt behavior infringe upon the peace and safety of the entire society? Almost any kind of behavior could be given a religious justification. If religious actions were held to be absolutely privileged, such behavior could thereby avoid regulation. Obviously the state in the interests of justice, harmony, and welfare must be able to limit even actions which claim religious justification—and even if they are known to be sincere.

But then the question must be asked whether this qualifies fatally all exercise of religious liberty. I do not believe it does, provided it is always understood that the state may regulate only actions, never the communication of a point of view. The state must act, indeed, if God is to be obeyed. The state may err in its actions, but, as many have pointed out, even the errors of the state may be corrected if there is constant freedom of the governed to criticize the government.

The absolute, the qualified absolute, and the qualified forms of religious liberty are all completely committed to religious liberty. The only limitations appear at the point of action.

2. The Problem of Religious Establishment

While mankind seems more committed to religious liberty today than ever before in its history (with religious persecution everywhere more on the defensive before the bar of world opinion), there is much less agreement about

190

whether the state should give special privileges to this or that religious group or to religious institutions in general. This is the question of religious establishment. In some countries, notably in the United States, this question often is raised by asking whether there should be separation of church and state. As a matter of fact, the number of societies which have *not* had some form of religious establishment is probably very small, whether one considers this from the historical perspective or that of contemporary national arrangements. Is the issue of religious establishment (or "separation of church and state") clarified by Protestant faith as understood in this volume?

Two things need to be said immediately. In the first place, it is now generally understood that religious liberty is the primary goal.[3] If religious establishment is to be criticized it is because of its negative effects upon religious liberty. Professor Wilber G. Katz, a noted American constitutional authority, explains this relationship in terms of American law as follows:

The basic American principle of church-state relations is not separation but religious liberty. This liberty includes freedom from government aid as well as freedom from restraint. Religious freedom has its limits, but they are not limits set by a principle of separation of church and state.[4]

The point gains added force when the Christian faith, rather than American principle, is taken as normative.

The second point is that there may be less inconsistency between religious establishment and religious liberty than is sometimes supposed. Indeed, there is probably more religious liberty in countries such as England and Sweden, both with established churches, than there is in some other militantly secular or anticlerical lands, such as Mexico or Haiti. (I have not used the Soviet Union as an illustration here because in that country Marxism may be considered an established religion in every meaningful sense of the term—an establishment which, furthermore, has severely limited religious freedom for non-Marxist religions.) Dr. Carrillo argues, in fact, that formal religious establishment is not at all inconsistent with full religious liberty, even though he believes establishment to pose certain dangers. "It seems obvious," he writes,

particularly concerning our problem, that countries which officially profess a particular religion *may have* a correct conception of religion liberty. We think, for instance, that the British understanding of religious freedom in the modern times is a perfect one, in spite of having an established church.[5]

Among the dangers of religious establishment he points to the following: the temptation to use religion for political unity, the possibility of restrictions being placed upon the established church itself, and the danger that if the established religion opposes religious liberty the government's policy will ultimately be affected. But these are seen as practical risks. In principle, he sees no necessary contradiction between freedom and establishment, and he records this as a moot point in contemporary ecumenical discussion.

One must agree that, *practically* speaking, there may be less inconsistency between freedom and establishment than is supposed (although it is astonishing to hear anybody refer to the British understanding of religious freedom as "a perfect one" in view of the difficulties of the Anglican church itself in securing official acceptance of changes in its liturgy by Parliament). But the grounds for rejecting religious establishment are theoretical, and theoretical understanding generally has important effects upon practice in the long run. Theoretically it should be clear that for the state to accord special privileges to one particular religious tradition, it must to that degree make a religious judgment: *for* the favored religion and *against* all others. We have already suggested that the determination of religious issues as matters of ultimate faith is not possible in the responsible state. While it is possible for people to act together through the state (even though some may dissent from the rightness of a policy), they have to do their believing one at a time. When the power of the state is used to undergird a particular form of belief or worship, the suggestion is clearly made that the issue of religious faith in that society is now a closed one. It is not the same thing as the state acting on the basis of majority judgment in the assurance that tomorrow the action may be reversed by the minority's becoming the majority. The reason why actions may be reversed is that the sources of action and the justification of action are held to be open questions. But if this, too, becomes a closed issue, there is no formal acknowledgment of the openness of every question and of the integrity of every member of the state as a person whose religious views must be respected equally with every other. When states with established churches are generous in their extension of religious liberty to other groups, the implication remains that dissenting views are not as worthy of expression; they are merely tolerated. This is to say, the state officially pronounces that of two persons only one of whom is a member of the established religion the views of that one are more worthy of a hearing than the views of the other. This is exactly the kind of thing the Protestant principle cannot permit. God can speak through anybody, and anybody can err. Established religion always flirts with idolatry, particularly when it becomes an instrument of national policy or a means to social unity.

I believe that religious establishment must be understood as a form of denial of religious liberty because of the relative advantages and disadvantages which it erects. To say that in some countries the disadvantages are but slight is only to say that the denial of religious liberty is a matter of degrees, when in principle it is wrong in any degree.

The ironic thing is that religious establishment, quite apart from these formal problems, is so often the very best way to destroy the inner meaning and vitality of the established church itself. One is hard put to decide whether establishment of one's church is to be preferred to persecution! Such Protestant writers as Franklin Littell, Dean Kelley, and Martin E. Marty have made this a vigorous point. In a stimulating recent book Marty suggests that American Protestantism is just now emerging from a kind of social or cultural "establishment" in which Protestantism has been enervated by being taken too much for granted.[6] He points out that Protestantism has been so much the cultural form of American society that it has been difficult for Protestants to confront people genuinely with Protestant ideas. Protestantism has been like the wallpaper of a room—very much in evidence but scarcely noticed. Now that pluralism is emerging, suggests Marty, Protestantism can be more like the furniture—something to be noticed and discussed. I do not want to push the argument too far, but the Protestant understanding of radically monotheistic worship would seem good preparation for a criticism of what establishment does to the purity of that worship.

Persons who favor establishment need to ask themselves serious questions. If they do not fear the effects of establishment upon their own faith when they represent the majority, they should ask how they would feel if a radically different, even contradictory, faith were established and they were required to support it. Who of us, for instance, is very happy with the Russian establishment of Marxism? How do we feel about state support for atheistic propaganda, for maintenance of anti-religious museums, for the indoctrination of children? Even if such establishment of atheism existed alongside perfect religious freedom, as it apparently does not do in Russia, the sheer pretension of the state's entry into the field of religion is much clearer to us when seen in that context than it is if the religion supported is not too different from our own.

Such objections relate to governmental establishment of religion and religious institutions as such. What about institutions which are but nominally or partially related to religious bodies and which the state desires to support for other, nonreligious reasons? In the United States the question of religious establishment is generally raised in this form. Institutions in the health, education, and welfare fields may usefully serve the interests of government even though they retain a relationship to a religious group. Often governments have believed that they could more efficiently serve the health, education, and welfare needs of their people by spending tax funds in support of such church-related agencies than they could be if attempting to develop similar public agencies from scratch. In the United States, for instance, programs of community self-help in the "war on poverty" under the Economic Opportunities Act have made considerable use of church-related agencies already at work in difficult urban and rural settings. Similarly, the American Peace Corps has occasionally worked with indigenous religious groups abroad, but special efforts have been made to guarantee that aid programs would not discriminate in any way on the basis of religion. The emerging new nations of Asia and Africa have sometimes simply supported Western missionary schools in some localities in lieu of developing their own schools. Such illustrations raise the question whether the objections to religious establishment extend to the support of church-related agencies whose primary functions are not religious.

I see no need for an absolute, legalistic rejection of all such support, provided that certain questions can be answered affirmatively: Is the agency in fact serving the public interest? Does the agency serve the public without arbitrary prejudice and discrimination, so that public funds are equally available for all within the specified category of need? Is everybody aware of the economic source of the agency's good works, so that the sponsoring religious body will not profit from the unmerited gratitude of beneficiaries of the program? Are governmental policy guidelines, designed to guarantee that the public interest is fulfilled, being honored responsibly by the agency and supervised adequately by government? Insofar as the agency provides opportunity for religious witness, is that opportunity equally available to all religious points of view? Do all religious groups have equal opportunity to sponsor agencies which will receive such governmental aid (that is, in designating which agencies are to be used, is the state non-discriminatory from a religious point of view)? Responsible adherence to such criteria might remove the legitimate objections to state support for religiously sponsored institutions where this promotes governmental efficiency in the use of its funds for nonreligious purposes.

The National Study Conference on Church and State, which was sponsored by the National Council of Churches in 1964, made a signal contribution along this line by suggesting such criteria for the offering of state aid to religious agencies. In its *General Findings* the Conference stated that

under some well-defined circumstances, government may legitimately support specific programs of church-affiliated health and welfare agencies. The sole purpose of any governmental policy in this respect must be the promotion of a clearly identifiable public interest as against a private interest of an individual or religious group. The important considerations here are (a) that the governmental programs must not be aimed primarily at the support of religious institutions or objectives, (b) that any support of church-affiliated agencies must be an incidental part of a large program directed to appropriate public interests, (c) that the agency does not discriminate on the basis of race, color, creed, or national origin, and (d) that reversionary clauses, limited to a fixed and reasonable period, be written into all contractual arrangements to insure that funds, buildings and equipment are not diverted from the purposes for which they were originally acquired.[7]

Special note should be taken of the inclusion of the word "creed" under part (c) in this statement. For a religious agency to agree not to discriminate on the basis of "creed" as a condition for receiving public funds is fairly close to saying that the agency must give up its religious character. Would this mean, then, a subtle but real denial of religious liberty by government? It must be remembered that the government does not require acceptance of its funds. This point was made in the *General Findings*.

Government must never coerce church-affiliated health, educational, or welfare agencies into acceptance of public support of any of their programs. Such coercion would constitute an unwarranted infringement of the freedom of church-affiliated agencies. However, so long as church-affiliated agencies have the freedom to accept or reject government support of any of their programs, it is not an unwarranted restriction of their discretion to require them to conform to governmentally-prescribed policy and program standards as a condition for voluntarily receiving the public support. Government must never abdicate its responsibility to protect the public interest in the expenditure of public funds.[8]

I believe this perspective to be a correct application of the idea of the responsible state to the problem of "religious establishment" which is presented by state support of church-related agencies.

Another question can be raised, however, which helps to define the problem of religious establishment still further. What if government establishes *all* religions, giving official recognition to all religious traditions and institutions and supporting their work with funds derived from taxation? As this proposal is sometimes put, it is government's duty to religion in recognition of the high and necessary role played by religion in every society. Surely there could be nothing improper in governmental support for all religions. As a matter of fact, this may be true! There may be little objection to religious establishment provided (1) it involves equal governmental recognition and support of all religious points of view, (2) it is understood that everybody has a religious point of view of some sort, and (3) organized religion is not subtly accorded any advantage over the religious activity of individuals who are not related to some organized religious group. But, of course, if religious establishment is not selective it is not really religious establishment. Generally those who support religious establishment for all religions really are not thinking so inclusively. They have in mind all Christian religions, or all Hebrew-Christian religions, or all theistic religions, or all recognized world religions, or all organized religions. But none of these categories is universally inclusive.

There *is* an important sense, however, in which the state must support religion when religion is defined in most inclusive terms. A responsible state must guarantee conditions which best undergird all religious inquiry and expression. It must be particularly concerned with creating opportunity for religious dialogue—again, in the most inclusive sense of the word. The distinction is not merely verbal. The case against establishment of religion can so easily drift into hostility to religious expression and organization or into a kind of officially encouraged indifferentism which is uneasy wherever ultimate questions are raised and ultimate answers ventured. Moreover, the conditions for religious dialogue are by no means easily guaranteed in complex modern civilizations. But I would argue that this is a positive duty of the state if it wants its members to be responsible in the fullest sense of the word and if it wants public discussion culminating in public policy consciously to examine the deepest wellsprings from which public policy can be derived. The provision of public forums for the full expression of opinion is a more urgent and complicated need than the simple provision of a Hyde Park, a Boston Common, or a Pershing Square. In modern life it extends deeply into the educational venture—a proposition to be examined shortly.

A few final comments may be made regarding the question of separation of church and state. The discussion to this point has probably encompassed the main concerns of those who use the expression most vigorously in America today. But there are some who view the expression itself with almost religious devotion. Taken *literally*, of course, the phrase "separation of church and state" is unthinkable, as is the Jeffersonian metaphor "a wall of separation between church and state" which has been quoted affirmatively by the U.S. Supreme Court. Since the state is society acting as a whole, the church would have to find a different society of which to be a part if it were to be totally separated from the state. Moreover, a situation would be unthinkable in which the state did not have power to regulate some of the material affairs of the church, however much that power ought to be exercised with restraint and with due respect for religious liberty.

Even applied metaphorically, the term poses problems. Those who use it should recognize that the new complexities of urban civilization unquestionably pose new problems which must be resolved in creative, not merely legalistic, ways. Despite such problems, however, I believe the phrase has served as a useful symbol for the state's commitment against religious establishment. Remembering always that such a metaphor is not to be taken propositionally or literally, it is a good reminder that the responsible state is one which does not accord preferential treatment to any religious tradition or institution in relation to others.

3. The Problem of Religious Education

It should not be surprising that some of the most complex and controversial issues of religious liberty and church-state relations in the modern world have accompanied the emergence of universal public school education. Education is a critically decisive aspect of culture, for it involves the transmission of man's traditions and heritages of knowledge, the development of intellectual capacity in the young, the criticism of old ideas and the examination of new ones. The fate of religious traditions and groups rests to a considerable degree upon their ability to be transmitted through educational means and to find appropriate criticism and interpretation from generation to generation. In primitive and not so primitive societies, religion has often borne sole or primary responsibility for all education, and "secular" learning has typically been transmitted in a fundamentally religious perspective. But this dependency of education upon religious institutions has changed astonishingly in the modern world. Within the past century—a century which has witnessed so many other revolutionary cultural developments and sociological changes—education has increasingly become a primarily political responsibility. To a large extent it has correspondingly come to be understood as a universal right and obligation, in the sense that the state must provide for and may require enrollment of the young in schools. Education as such, of course, is ubiquitous in all human culture and has been a part of social structure from the beginning of history. But this new role of the state presents some interesting dilemmas to the student of religious liberty.

These dilemmas are presented in different ways in various countries, and the American experience is particularly important, partly because this country has largely pioneered in the modern commitment to universal, free, compulsory public school participation, and partly because it has also had a deep tradition of commitment to religious liberty. It is very important to remember that American national traditions of religious liberty and separation of church and state antedate the American development of universal public school education. (The first state to establish compulsory public school education was Massachusetts, in 1842, a full half-century *after* the adoption of the U.S. Constitution.) This is to say that the founders of the republic may not be supposed to have had the arena of education in mind when they gave shape to the traditions of freedom in a Bill of Rights. They assumed education to be private and local. They would have assumed, moreover, its inclusion of religious elements. As Canon Stokes put it, "most of the leaders expected the old endowed schools and the churches to continue to provide all necessary education outside the home, and even where new schools were started or old academies given state aid it was generally assumed that religious instruction would be continued." [9]

In America, therefore, the establishment of policy regarding religion in state-supported education has presented unanticipated problems which have grown along with education itself. Had America remained generally Protestant in culture, Protestant elements in public school instruction and activity might not have been given particular notice (and such elements would not likely have led to judicial and legislative battles). But with the vast growth of the country and its increasing pluralism, the generally Protestant heritage of the schools (a carry-over from the distinctively religious common schools of the colonial and early national periods) became an irritant to those not sharing that heritage. This has led to the closest evaluation of the role of religion in education in terms of principles of religious liberty and the nonestablishment of religion.

In formal terms the basic problem has seemed clear enough. If the state sponsors, administers, and finances the schools, are they not agencies of the state? If they are agencies of the state, is not their teaching of religion a form of religious establishment? Does it not, moreover, infringe upon the religious liberty of those whose religious traditions and commitments are alien to those taught by the schools?

Various solutions have been proposed to meet this problem without sacrificing the religious instruction which many people recognize to be vital to the life of the churches. In a surprisingly large number of communities, particularly in the predominantly Protestant regions of the Midwest and South and especially in smaller communities, the problem is simply ignored. Schools frankly continue to conduct devotional exercises (sometimes including weekly chapel services), stanchly celebrate religious holidays, and provide religious instruction. They thus provide a rough parallel to some predominantly Roman Catholic countries where the public schools assume and help transmit Roman Catholic tradition. In other areas different solutions have been tried. About a generation ago considerable support was given to the idea that, while state-supported schools could not provide instruction and worship in a simple tradition, they could seek out the "common core" of all religious (or of Hebrew-Christian) traditions and make it the basis for the school's approach. But this, of course, overlooked the fact that many religious views could not well be included. Moreover, people began to recognize that the lowest common denominator even among Hebrew-Christian traditions could hardly be said to do honest justice to any of those traditions. Recognizing this, there was some experimentation in cooperative arrangements between church and school, with the schools releasing pupils for instruction in the churches for specified periods (the "released-time" movement). This movement led to various court tests, the effect of which was to legalize the approach provided the programs were not held on the school premises. The approach has never been much of a success, however, partly because not much time has generally been allotted, partly because

203

churches have had difficulty in the financial support of the program, and partly because the approach seemed to accept as an assumption that in the public school classroom itself, where the real educational venture occurs, religion is indeed off limits.

More recently there has been some experimentation with "shared-time" arrangements, whereby church sponsored schools teach the children in those subject-matter areas considered sensitive from the religious point of view and the public schools deal with everything else. Despite administrative difficulties, the arrangement seems to be constitutional.[10] It may have creative possibilities which bear watching. (The 1964 National Study Conference on Church and State gave strong support to "shared-time" as a method of dealing with religious education.) This approach may, moreover, resolve some of the dilemmas facing Roman Catholic parochial schools by providing a way whereby public education can shoulder part of the financial burden without compromising with religious establishment. It might also help break down the educational segregation of Roman Catholic youngsters from Protestants and others. The difficulty remains, however, that religion has been removed from the public schools, with the implication that nothing has been sacrificed educationally in the process and that the state has correctly applied its commitment to religious liberty. Within educational circles there is notable reluctance to venture very much in any direction respecting religion, and the result can probably be recorded as the growing secularity of public school education in the United States taken as a whole. In part (and with the reservation mentioned below), this process has seemed to be accelerated greatly by recent Supreme Court decisions prohibiting the corporate recitation of prayer and devotional Bible reading in public schools.

A somewhat abortive effort to lead the way out of this morass was recently suggested by Professor John Bennett, who argued that while "the state makes possible the public school" it "is an expression of the community and not a mere instrument of the state." [11] He uses the word "community" in this context "to refer not to the local political unit but to society, in contrast to the state." The schools, thus, might well be left free to reflect the religious traditions of the community and to provide them their needed educational outlet without involving religious establishment or the denial of religious liberty. This solution does logically express the American tradition of the common school (which antedates the public school system and even nationhood), and it also recognizes that the state may not simply be equated with the community or society. But, as he has used these terms, the distinction between society and state may be insupportable. When "society" acts as a whole to sponsor schools and to support them through (coercive) taxation and (coercive) attendance requirements, it *is* the state. Nevertheless, Professor Bennett has expressed a valid concern. Something is wrong when the state has, in effect, preempted sponsorship of the schools and then simply driven religion out of education.

I believe that the Protestant perspective developed in this book provides clarification in this situation; a clarification which may have applicability not only in the United States but also in other countries which similarly must resolve the problem of religion in state schools. In that perspective, religion (as each man's perception of the ultimate) must be taken seriously wherever it is encountered. Education must include examination of the place of religion in human life aid culture if it is to be education in any real sense of the word. At the same time, that perspective would remain properly skeptical about any one religious tradition or point of view exhausting the possibilities of authentic witness to ultimate truth and value. In that perspective, worship or "devotions" are clearly not the proper business of the state school, for worship implies commitments which cannot be assumed and excludes persons whose religion must not be prejudiced as being of less value by the state school. (In this sense, the U.S. Supreme Court decisions of 1961 and 1963 which ban prescribed prayer and devotional Bible readings are clearly correct, and it may be anticipated that the ban will be extended to include such things as baccalaureate worship services for graduates.) But on the other hand it clearly seems legitimate and even necessary for the schools to deal with religion in their curricula if they do not prejudice religious traditions or expressions, nor seek commitment. This perspective would be similar to those who argue, on grounds of the U.S. Constitution, that it is proper for the schools to teach *about* religion.[12] In the 1963 Abington case, the Supreme Court itself expressed this judgment by asserting that

one's education is not complete without a study of comparative religion or the history of religion and its relationship to the advancement of civilization. It certainly may be said that the Bible is worthy of study for its literary and historical qualities. Nothing we have said here indicates that such study of the Bible or of religion, when presented objectively as part of a secular program of education, may not be effected consistent with the First Amendment.[13]

In a concurring opinion, Justice Brennan stated that

the holding of the Court today plainly does not foreclose teaching *about* the Holy Scriptures or about the differences between religious sects in classes in literature or history. In-deed, whether or not the Bible is involved, it would be im-possible to teach meaningfully many subjects in the social sciences or the humanities without some mention of religion.[14]

Religion, thus, does not need to be avoided by the schools. It can be taken seriously by the state. But the problems of religious liberty and religious establishment are para-doxically avoided because the state takes the religion of *everybody* seriously.

The question whether religion should be taken serious-ly in this way is an issue which sharply divides those who oppose religion in the schools for the sake of religious liberty. To the secularist, religion should be avoided be-cause he believes that it is not to be taken seriously. (Some secularists doubtless believe that one of the main functions of education is to help people find liberation from re-ligion.) But to the Protestant Christian, religious com-mitment by the schools is to be avoided precisely because the religion of all is to be taken seriously (again on the as-sumption that the sovereign God can work in and through all in ways that it would be blasphemous for any to pre-judge). But excluding religious commitments by the schools, the Protestant Christian can enthusiastically en-dorse a study of religion which is sensitive and sympathetic to all its manifestations and properly honest and critical with its points of vulnerability. I believe that those who are entirely opposed even to the teaching about religion in the schools have little real respect for the personalities of the students, for they take with little seriousness that which is most important to the students themselves—their ulti-mate commitments and most treasured traditions.

To establish the formal rightness, even the necessity, of the inclusion of religious content in education as a matter of policy does not, of course, provide much guidance as to how this can be worked out at different age levels and in relation to different subject matters. It would be presumptuous to venture many suggestions here.[15] I am mainly concerned that education take every religious point of view seriously in the expectancy that it does indeed have something to contribute, and that religion not be avoided out of a misdirected fear of religious establishment. Practically, the task is to encourage every child and young person's religious self-respect and his appreciation and sensitivity to others. Ultimately, the task is also to encourage the development of every student's critical capacities as well. It must be insisted that *this is possible, desirable, and necessary in some sense at every level of education from the elementary schools through the university.* In principle and in practice, the defensive conspiracy of silence concerning religion must be ended wherever education desires to be more than trivial—provided, always, that education is not considered to be the same thing as worship and provided that all religious manifestations are taken seriously, if only because those who express them are taken seriously as persons.

At the lower levels of education, the task would seem to require greater sensitivity on the part of the teacher. The teacher must be especially careful not to challenge the religious faith of the child because of the high esteem and authority which the teacher's role commands. Rather, the teacher might encourage awareness in the classroom of the different backgrounds from which the children come and appreciation of those with different traditions. The higher the level of education, the more can the intellectual independence of the student be assumed, and therefore the wider the possibilities of dialogue which become opened. On the college or university level I see no reason why the full thrust of religious dialogue should not be encouraged, with the fullest possible examination given to different religious traditions and to such disciplines as sociology of religion and psychology of religion. The dialogue can and should be open to the most radical challenging of any idea, but under the rule that no idea has been challenged properly unless it has had the fullest opportunity for presentation and counter-challenge.

The schools are thus seen as providing more than a "training" experience to prepare the young for vocational pursuits in their adult life. They become a forum for the dialogue of the democratic society which prepares the young for mature participation in that society. In this perspective we may be speaking of, more even than teaching "about," religion, a phrase which has never appealed to me because it implies that religion is a "thing" about which the sophisticated person will have knowledge just as he does about other "things." In the perspective of this book religion is at the heart of all life. Its *manifestations* can and should be examined as "things" are examined, but it is understood that religion is what is at the center of all profound dialogue. The role of religion in education should point in this more dynamic, living, vital direction. Commitment by public education to any one tradition (or commitment by public education *against* any one tradition) is plainly wrong, in violation of religious liberty, and a grave risk of idolatry. Avoidance of religious subjects and issues is similarly a grotesque caricature of religious liberty which denies that which gives meaning to the principle itself. Acceptance of the difficult but challenging educational task of stimulating religious awareness and dialogue is, however, in the finest sense faithful to the inner intention of religious liberty as we have explored it in these pages.

4. The Problem of Religious Schools

Issues of religious liberty and religious establishment become intwined in peculiar ways in the problem of educational institutions and programs sponsored by religious groups. The issue of religious liberty centers in the question of the right of religious groups to establish educational programs and institutions which (a) supplement or (b) serve as a substitute for public school education. The issue of religious establishment is raised in the question whether such programs or institutions ought properly to be supported by the state. These issues are particularly real in the United States where a large-scale Roman Catholic parochial school program has developed alongside public school education, posing the question of whether this program should to some extent be financed by government. But such issues are more universal, even in societies which have not yet felt their force—partly because of the nearly universal development of public school education and partly because few religious groups could remain satisfied with such exposure to their traditions as the children might receive through the public schools (in the manner discussed in the preceding section).

The right of groups to *supplement* public school education seems indisputable if religious liberty has any meaning at all. This right could be considered a "qualified absolute" one in the sense in which we used that term in the first section of this chapter. From the point of view of the religious group, this right must also be understood as a practical necessity. If public school education must take religion seriously and afford it proper consideration in an atmosphere of free discussion, it is clear that there would not be time for a child to receive that thorough grounding in his own tradition which would make his own full participation in dialogue meaningful. There would not be time for the schools to give adequate exposure to all traditions and points of view, nor could it be expected that the instruction would have the same competence.[16]

I have already expressed some skepticism about the typical "released time" program. But it must be said that the availability of time for churches to conduct supplementary programs can no longer be taken for granted. If the freedom of churches to do a thorough job of grounding their children in their traditions and point of view is to be taken seriously, the freedom becomes meaningful only if the time available to do this is also optimum time —not a "tag-end" situation which places undue strains upon the attention and energies of the children and upon their normal family life at home. We should be perfectly willing to leave the determination of this kind of issue to the educational experts, provided they recognize the legitimacy of the concern of parents and religious groups. It is not reasonable for them to assume that they "own" all of the child's optimum learning time. My own judgment would be that, in situations where weekends are free and after-school time is not overburdened with school sponsored activities and homework assignments, church groups may well have all the freedom they need without the dubious features of "released time." But the growth of educational programs in directions of enrichment activity after school, on weekends, and during the summer months requires that great sensitivity be exercised by public school officials to be sure that neither explicitly nor subtly are they infringing upon aspects of the child's development for which they are not prepared to assume responsibility.[17]

The right of religious groups to provide a *substitute* for public school instruction raises more serious questions. In the United States this right has been affirmed in the 1925 Supreme Court decision, *Pierce v. Society and Sisters*

—a decision which Leo Pfeffer has described as the "Magna Carta of private schools in America and perhaps as well the Magna Carta of cultural pluralism." [18] According to the Pierce decision,

The fundamental theory of liberty upon which all governments in this Union repose excludes any general power of the State to standardize its children by forcing them to accept instruction from public teachers only. The child is not the mere creature of the State; those who nurture him and direct his destiny have the right, coupled with the high duty, to recognize and prepare him for additional obligations.

By this ruling the court voided an Oregon law requiring all children to attend public schools even if private and parochial schools of equal competence were available. It should be noted that the ruling rested, not on the rights of private or parochial schools in themselves, but on the rights of parents in the education of their children. This right being prior to that of the state, the parents of children must be free to place their children in private or parochial schools in fulfillment of their educational obligations.

The basis of this decision by the U.S. Supreme Court rather closely parallels the logic of Pope Pius XI's encyclical *Divini Illius Magistri,* in which the pope also considers the educational responsibility of the parent to be prior to that of the state: "God directly communicates to the family, in the natural order, fecundity, which is the principle of life, and hence also the principle of education to life, together with authority, the principle of order." The family "holds directly from the Creator the mission and hence the right to educate the offspring, a right inalienable because inseparably joined to the strict obligation, a right anterior to any right whatever of civil society and of the State."

While both the Court and the pope stated the case for parental rights in the strongest language, both also recognize that such rights are not absolute. The state may properly intervene in the nurture of children despite the opposition of parents if such action is necessary to protect the common good and the rights of the children themselves. Pius XI put it this way: "It also belongs to the State to protect the rights of the child itself when the parents are found wanting either physically or morally in this respect, whether by default, incapacity, or misconduct." And the Court similarly limited the educational rights of parents and of private schools by its explicit provision that

no question is raised concerning the power of the State reasonably to regulate all schools, to inspect, supervise and examine them, their teachers and pupils; to require that all children of proper age attend some school, that teachers shall be of good moral character and patriotic disposition, that certain studies plainly essential to good citizenship must be taught, and that nothing be taught which is manifestly inimical to the public welfare.

If, indeed, the rights of parents or church in the education of children were held to be absolute, the state might find itself sacrificing the rights both of the children and of the broader community. In the case of education the state has properly assumed responsibility for certain standards which follow from the responsibility of the state to secure justice for all its citizens. The possibility that some parents might not wish to have their children educated or that they might wish to educate them without exposing them to, say, history, mathematics, or literature, would not excuse the state from its obligation to protect the child from the ignorant or warped perspective of its parents any more than from cruel and inhuman parental treatment. The point is illustrated by legal decision permitting the state to intervene to require blood transfusions for children despite religious objections of parents.

While children are not citizens in the full sense of the word, and while it would be unspeakable folly for the state not to recognize the right and obligation of parents to nurture their own children, it remains that the *civil* rights of the child are defined and guaranteed by the state, not by his parents. Respecting education, moreover, the civil rights of the child in the responsible state include preparation for life in a civilized community. The precise meaning of adequate preparation will, of course, be variously defined according to historical circumstances. One would expect the state's educational standards to be under constant development and change. But religious or parental immunity from such standards can hardly be classified as an absolute right. As hypothetical illustrations, if religious schools were created for the partial purpose of providing religious insulation from modern science, if they were to bombard pupils throughout their formal education with factually incorrect data and highly biased interpretations, the pupils would suffer serious handicaps in later life, and society would be deprived of the full contributions which they might otherwise be expected to make in later life. By interfering with such schools, the state might be accused of attempting to standardize its pupils. But insisting that the young be equipped to deal with life in the modern world is not the same thing as standardizing their viewpoints. Indeed, part of what I mean by "equipping the young" is equipping them to participate in dialogue by expressing and defending their own unique perspectives on life.

This brings us back to the specific problem of religious schools. As a substitute for public instruction one could argue that such schools risk failure in one decisive particular, namely, that they may not prepare their students for the broad appreciation of traditions different from their own which is essential to the dialogue of a responsible society. This is partly because such schools generally lack sociological diversity. A student may not be able to have direct social contact with others who have a different viewpoint. It is also partly because instruction is likely to prejudge all other religious points of view, thus undermining that combination of respect, skepticism, and expectancy on the basis of which genuine dialogue is founded.

Should private religious schools, then, be prohibited as substitutes for public education?

I am unwilling to press the argument to such an extreme for two reasons. First, since it has *not* been demonstrated factually that *religious* schools are unable to prepare their pupils for effective life in a democratic society, and barring such a demonstration, the presumption should lie with freedom. Secondly, it has *not* been demonstrated factually that *public* schools can provide the essential religious grounding which is felt to be necessary by many religious groups, and barring *that* demonstration, the presumption must support the efforts of private groups to fill this gap. I am unwilling, however, to adopt one argument which some have employed as justification for religious schools. That is the contention that the public schools are pre-committed to a "secularist" philosophy and that students who do not wish to study under the presuppositions of this particular philosophy therefore should have free-

215

dom to study within the framework of a more compatible point of view. Dean Robert F. Drinan of the Boston College School of Law has presented this view in a fairly characteristic way. He argues that public schools are, in effect, a type of religious establishment—the establishment of the attitude that religion is irrelevant:

The secularized public school meets and treats its students only as future citizens. Their religious or spiritual beliefs are to be regarded as irrelevant and hence unimportant with respect to the entire educational process. It is this basic disregard of the great ideas and religious aspirations in the lives of the students in a public school which is the gravamen of the religionist's complaint. To the believer—at least to many believers—the silent assumption by the public school that religion in any meaningful sense is irrelevant to the educational process amounts to an official establishment of secular values.[19]

He continues by asking how it is possible ("in a nation whose law knows no heresy and whose legal institutions support no orthodoxy") for one "to reject the contention made by a substantial minority of citizens that the tax-supported school, by its silent disregard of religion, thereby promotes irreligion." But this portrait of "secular public schools" is also highly inconsistent with our discussion of religion in the public schools in the responsible state. When public schools have "disregard of the great ideas and religious aspirations in the lives of the students" and assume, silently or explicitly, "that religion in any meaningful sense is irrelevant to the educational process," the schools themselves violate their true nature and purpose as seen in this book. Would Dean Drinan be willing to surrender his case for a parochial school system if, in practice as well as in theory, the public schools were to take religion seriously? Would he feel that exposure to other religious perspectives in an atmosphere conducive to appreciation and dialogue would be destructive to the religious faith of children? These questions are not raised in an argumentative spirit (because he has pointed to a real problem), but to clarify the implications of the view that, for religious reasons, a religious group should be responsible for *all* the education of its young.

Granted, however, the qualified right of religious groups to provide private schools in lieu of the public school system, the question remains whether it is necessary or proper for the state to finance all or part of the cost of such schools. This has become a very heated issue in American society and one which may not finally be resolved for a long time. The case for public support of religious schools has been summarized by Dean Drinan in the following way:

1. The fully accredited private school has important public dimensions in that it carries out the secular goals of the state; because of this semi-public status conferred on the private school this institution has some claim to share in the public funds set aside by the state for the education of all of its future citizens.

2. Public welfare benefits surely include secular education, and by the rulings in *Cochran* and *Everson* the benefits extended by the state to all citizens may not be denied to anyone because of his religious faith or lack of it.

3. In the distribution of these public welfare benefits no Supreme Court opinion has held that the only constitutional formula is one which prevents even some incidental aid to religion.

4. In view of clear Supreme Court rulings precluding sectarian teaching and religious practices in public schools it can be persuasively argued that the granting of funds only to the public school is a violation of the establishment clause because such a policy endorses and prefers one educational and philosophical orthodoxy over all others.[20]

In a similar vein, Fr. Murray has held that "the principle of distributive justice would require that a proportionately just measure of public support should be available to such schools as serve the public cause of popular education, whether these schools be specifically religious in their affiliation and orientation, or not." [21]

It is important for Protestants to try to understand this point of view. The argument seems to be that in the distribution of political benefits, justice requires that those benefits be equally available to all persons in the class to whom the benefits apply. (Otherwise the state will have favored some of its citizens over others and violated the norm of equality.) Public school education, however, restricts the benefit of education to those whose religious orientation is favorable to (or at least not offended by) the secularism of such schools. Similarly, it is prejudicial to those whose religious faith precludes acceptance of the benefit in the form in which it is proffered by the state. We would have the same problem, for instance, if the state were to provide free meat for all its citizens, but specify that the form should be pork—thus creating obvious difficulties for orthodox Jewish citizens; or, if the state were to provide free liquor, thus prejudicing the situation for many Methodists, Baptists, and other abstaining groups.

The application of such an argument to support public financing of religious schools seems to require acceptance of three assumptions: One must assume, first, that while religious schools are admittedly different they fulfill the educational requirements of the state—that is, they are a form of *educational* benefit, not some other *kind* of benefit. One must secondly assume that the public school form of the educational benefit is more prejudicial to some religious groups than it is to others. And one must finally assume that the granting of religious exemptions from general law requires the state also to finance the exercise of such exemptions (a principle which certainly has not been accepted in other areas, such as the military draft). The principle itself is disputable on the grounds of the uncertainty of the last assumption. But the first two assumptions raise the questions which I wish to pursue here.

First, it seems to me that there is no proper ground for arguing that the public school system, if it takes seriously the points which were made in section three of this chapter, is more or less prejudicial to any religious group— except insofar as a religious group seeks to insulate itself from contact with the rest of society. In principle Roman Catholicism, Protestantism, Mormonism, Buddhism, Judaism, Hinduism, all should feel the public schools to be sympathetic to their traditions and sensitive to the convictions of their adherents.

Secondly, however, the assumption that religious schools will indeed fulfill the state's educational requirements leads one to the observation that in doing so they will have become the agents of the state. If such schools are to receive tax funds they become agencies of the state to an even greater degree. They become responsible to the state in two ways: first, through administration of those minima of education which the state holds to be the necessary and just due of every one of its children, and second, through the administration of funds collected by the state from all the people. If they are, in fact, agencies of the state, what they do and the way they do it become everybody's business. All the criteria suggested above in the section on religious establishment, including nondiscrimination on the basis of race, color, or *creed,* would have to be made applicable. As administrator of funds collected from all the people, any religious organization would have to be responsible to all the people. And in the administration of such funds, persons could not be excluded from religious schools or discriminated against within its program because of their own religious affiliations and convictions. That is to say, their religious policy would then have to approximate that of the public schools. In principle it might thus be possible for religious schools and colleges to receive tax support. But if they are to assume their proper responsibility, then as agencies of the state it is doubtful that their *raison d' être* as religious schools could retain much meaning.

For this reason I consider that policy in the area of education the wisest which (1) generally restricts public funds to explicitly public institutions (except in situations where specific "purchase of services" is indicated or where direct benefits can be provided for the physical welfare of children), which (2) concentrates upon creative teaching about religion in public schools in such a way that all viewpoints are explored and taken seriously, and which (3) makes due provision of opportunity for the deeper instruction in a given religious viewpoint through special enrichment programs, "released time," and "shared time." In the long run, the best solution for the financial dilemmas of American Roman Catholic parochial schools may well be the "shared time" arrangement. This concept clearly provides for the separation of "secular" subject matter which fulfills state requirements from religious subject matter—with state and church respectively responsible for the financing and administration of each. This solution, moreover, might provide more opportunity for children of different religious backgrouds to get to know one another as persons.

5. The Problem of Religion and Political Action

Religion cannot be divorced from the political life of the community. Indeed, the history of Christianity emphatically underscores concern for relevance in the political arena, for in almost every age Christians and Christian churches have sought to influence politics in obedience to divine command. During the past century, American Protestantism, along with Christian bodies all over the world, has become increasingly conscious of its political obligation. Today it would be difficult to locate a theologian who would argue in principle that the Christian should in no way attempt to influence the course of political events. Despite this fact, however, the doctrines of religious liberty and separation of church and state have sometimes been employed to condemn specific political attitudes or involvements of Christian individuals and churches. What considerations should govern the policy of Christians in relation to this problem?

First, from the point of view of the responsible state, it is clearly understood that religion permeates politics through and through, for the religious faith of every citizen substantially forms the basis of his actions. This may even be true when people behave selfishly in the political decisions they make, for selfishness generally presupposes a form of idolatrous worship. The responsible state is responsible precisely to the extent its political institutions enable persons to express their deepest values and to act upon them in order to affect the policies of the state. Furthermore, the responsible state by definition is one which respects the religious integrity of each of its citizens and accords no more a priori power to one than to another.

Secondly, however, from the theological viewpoint of Protestant faith, it is primarily through the obedient action of faithful men that the sovereign God is enabled to act directly in human history. As we remarked earlier, the responsible state is the state in which God is best able to express his sovereignty, for in this kind of political order men confront fewer unnatural impediments to their witness and obedience to God. This is not to say that a responsible state may not, through the hardness of its people's hearts, frustrate the will of God. It may do so even more than a monarchy under a wise and compassionate king. But the form of the responsible state gives to every man the opportunity to be a wise and compassionate king, and the sphere of God's sovereignty is thus immeasurably enlarged and enriched. Moreover, even foolish political action can be reversed provided the structures of political responsibility are not impaired. In obedience to God, if God is genuinely and faithfully worshiped, the Christian *must* witness and act, and his witness and action must direct itself toward helping shape the things which society does when it acts as a whole. This possibility means that the Christian brings to political discussion unique insights into the inner meaning of justice which he seeks to help actualize in the political order.

Occasionally, the critic of Christian political action will admit this much but still insist that Christian political action should remain on the *individual* level. The supposition is that the proper role of the church is to change the hearts and minds of its individual members—not to act corporately. There is this much truth in the view: the church, in a responsible state, never becomes a political structure which is capable of exercising political power without responsibility to the whole society. It would be irresponsible for a religious body or a religious official to exercise political power ex officio.

But granted this, there are two ways in which the church may and must act politically. First, it has the opportunity and obligation to be in itself a dialogue concerning the relevance of Christian faith to the main issues of the day. In this sense, it should "educate" its members, although from the Protestant viewpoint it might better be said that the church represents members educating *one another* under the guidance of the Holy Spirit. Such a church takes seriously the direct access of God to each of its members, and it takes proper note of the sin and error which also can becloud the judgment of even its most honored leaders. Moreover, it takes seriously the areas of special competence of its members. The clergy are apt to have particular insight into the nuances of meaning in Scripture and theology, but such insight is no substitute for technical competence. On the other hand, technical competence alone never settles questions within the church, for technical competence can be made to serve quite pagan gods —as the scientists of the Third Reich demonstrated overwell. Dean Muelder describes this internal dialogue of the church and the peculiar contributions of the layman:

In no area of ministry is the life of the laity more directly involved than in the political realm. To guide them in their decisions the message of Christianity should throw a searchlight on the actual facts of the existing situation and reveal the concrete consequences of political behavior. Though the church as such expresses in its social doctrine no special competence in the technical sphere, yet spiritual principles have to find expression through the technical sphere. Only through an adequate conception of the teamwork of the whole church, including clergy and laity, can Christ be interpreted in terms of deeds.[22]

In harmony with this, the hallmark of ecumenical social witness in the twentieth century has been dialogue on the highest level among theologians and experts of the greatest competence in areas of technical concern. It is not generally enough understood by Christians that the social statements and documents produced by the World Council of Churches and the regional and national councils of churches typically reflect such technical as well as theological competence. While such statements and documents cannot, at peril of idolatry, be followed slavishly, their high quality renders them uniquely valuable as points of departure for further reflection by individual Christians and further dialogue within the churches. The same thing can be said about the great papal social encyclicals of the Roman Catholic Church. These documents also reflect considerable advance preparation by numerous scholars and experts, although the assumptions which lie behind the encyclicals are altogether more authoritarian than those upon which Protestant and Eastern Orthodox pronouncements are based.

The other way in which it is proper for the churches to act politically is through their direct witness to society and leaders outside the church. I have in mind here both the public pronouncements intended for general reading and direct "lobbying" activities which attempt to influence decision-makers in the centers of power. Of course churches run risks when they inject themselves as churches directly into political discussion, for they must expect to receive the same "rough and tumble" which others receive in the political arena. All the same, there is no valid reason *in principle* why churches should be restricted from entry into that arena in the same manner as other kinds of groups. It is ironic that opponents of church involvement in political debate are so often quite uncritical of organized efforts by the church's opponents on given issues. Presumably Christians are supposed to fight their political battles as heroic individuals, without the strength of organization and strategy, while their opponents are given leave to coordinate their efforts however they will. In the highly complex civilization which is emerging all over the world, political effectiveness increasingly requires organization, planning, and strategy. Even the opponents of direct church action are more likely to approve such action when it accords with their own firmest convictions. For instance, in some areas of the United States the church may be condemned for violating separation of church and state if it attempts to support civil rights laws. But it may be heartily approved when it supports laws regulating and prohibiting sale of liquor, gambling, and prostitution.[23] In principle, the church should always feel free to act corporately in the political arena.

In doing so, however, it wisely observes several limitations. If the church becomes a political party, its witness to transcendent values will inevitably be weakened by the compromises which are always a part of the political process. Moreover, it then limits the sphere of its effective political action to those who share a common faith tradition and it encourages the intermingling of religious competition with conflict over political issues. Also, it is unwise for the church to speak and act with respect to too many specific issues and generally with respect to particular candidates for office. Its witness should be reserved for those crucial and clear issues upon which many lesser issues may turn. While it may in principle support or oppose particular candidates, to do so risks great ambiguity and implies endorsement of the weaknesses as well as the strengths of particular candidates. It should reserve its witness for those issues where it can clearly relate the problem to the Christian faith—in such a way that there is no doubt in anybody's mind that the church is speaking and acting with integrity. It wisely does not *require* its members to follow its witness and action as a condition of their continued membership. I do not say that it *must* not. In a responsible state, if people wish to follow the dictates of a church in political matters, they are perfectly free to do so. Moreover, some issues may be so clear that as a matter of church discipline it is proper to insist upon specified actions. But the church should be very slow with such judgments, for God may be saying something through the dissenter which both church and society need to hear. The responsible state is well served by churches and other associations which are likewise democratic in character.

The church and individual Christians have no guarantee of the rightness of their position in political matters. This is a risk built into the very nature of human finitude, and it must be accepted as the price of all human witness and action. Realization of human finitude should cause Christians to avoid making an idol out of any social solution, however clear the case for its acceptance may be. But to accept the risk is to acknowledge still more the urgency of judgment and action. The world desperately needs the sensitive insight of Christians and the corporate witness of the church respecting the grave needs and dangers which it faces. In faithfulness to the sovereign God, Christians and churches must not fail to respond.

NOTES

[1] *The Basis of Religious Liberty*, pp. 20-26.
[2] Quoted by Leo Pfeffer, *Creeds in Competition* (New York: Harper & Row, 1958), pp. 161-62.
[3] Although the problem of religious liberty must be considered the primary consideration in a discussion of religious establishment, it

should not be forgotten that serious problems are also raised whenever an ecclesiastical power is permitted to dominate the political process from outside the normal channels of political influence available to other citizens and groups. Privileged power of this kind, whether it derive from religious or economic sources, undermines the integrity of responsible government.

[4] "The Case for Religious Liberty," in *Religion in America,* p. 115.

[5] *The Basis of Religious Liberty,* p. 51.

[6] *Second Chance for American Protestants* (New York: Harper & Row, 1963).

[7] The *General Findings* of the conference were its principle product. They have been published in various places, including *A Journal of Church and State,* CLI (1964), 147-53. The quotation is at p. 151. It should be noted here that the philosophy reflected in this quotation was especially dependent upon a proposal outlined in a paper by Dr. W. Astor Kirk. He was, moreover, responsible for the specific insertion of the word "creed" in the series following (c) by his actions on the floor as a delegate. To my knowledge, Dr. Kirk's brief paper remains unpublished as such.

[8] *General Findings,* p. 152.

[9] Anson Phelps Stokes, *Church and State in the United States* (New York: Harper and Brothers, 1950), II, 48-49.

[10] Cf. Wilber G. Katz, "Note on the Constitutionality of Shared Time," in Donald A. Giannella (ed.), *Religion and the Public Order, 1964* (Chicago: University of Chicago Press, 1965), pp. 85-95.

[11] "Absolutism in the Supreme Court," *Christianity and Crisis,* XXII, No. 14 (1962), p. 135.

[12] Cf. the excellent discussion by Katz in *Religion and American Constitutions* (Evanston: Northwestern University Press, 1964), pp. 33-56, and Paul A. Freund's analysis of the legal issues in Paul A. Freund and Robert Ulich, *Religion and the Public Schools* (Cambridge, Mass.: Harvard University Press, 1965), pp. 3-24.

[13] *School District of Abington Township v. Schempp,* 374 U.S. 225 (1963).

[14] *Ibid.,* p. 300.

[15] A number of creative suggestions appear in James E. Loder, *Religion and the Public Schools* (New York: Association Press Reflection Book, 1965). See esp. chap. 4, "Religious Literacy Versus Religious Indoctrination." See also Robert Ulich's discussion of "The Educational Issue" in *Religion and the Public Schools,* pp. 27-54.

[16] The competence of public school teachers in dealing with religion would, of course, be enhanced greatly if this aspect of their

own training were given more attention by the schools of education. Teacher training cannot guarantee the fitness of attitudes, but it can certainly assure exposure to much more information concerning religious traditions than most teachers currently seem to have.

[17] As a practical suggestion, it seems possible to me that specialized religious instruction could be incorporated into public school "enrichment" periods, even religious instruction that is thoroughly committed and accompanied by experiences of worship, *provided* that (a) all points of view are given access to this privilege without prejudice to any, and (b) no pupil is coerced to participate or not participate in any such program. In such a situation the schools would simply be providing a platform or forum—something which is faithful in the deepest sense to the concept of a responsible state.

[18] *Creeds in Competition,* p. 83.

[19] "The Constitutionality of Public Aid to Parochial Schools," in Dallin H. Oaks (ed.), *The Wall Between Church and State* (Chicago University of Chicago Press, 1963), pp. 69-70.

[20] *Ibid.,* pp. 71-72.

[21] *We Hold These Truths,* p. 146.

[22] "Christian Social Witness in the Modern State" (one of his 1962 Colliver Lectures at the University of the Pacific, unpublished).

[23] Some empirical evidence of this sort of inconsistency is provided by a 1962 survey of the opinions on Church-State matters of Protestant clergymen in Northern California. Among other things, these ministers were asked which of several specified issues a churchman "acting as a churchman" could properly discuss with governmental officials. Of 1,226 questionnaires returned, 1,117 checked "The churchman's opposition to gambling, liquor, prostitution, etc." Only 731 indicated "the churchman's support for foreign aid." Still fewer (445) considered it proper to discuss specific candidates for office (but see my discussion of this issue below). On a related question about what "a minister may properly use the pulpit to express his beliefs about," 365 checked "the value of Capitalism," while 297 checked "the value of Socialism." 637 indicated "the need for prohibition," 760 checked "the threat of Communism," and 751 checked "the rights of unpopular groups." (1,164 checked "the importance of serving God daily"!) The various options on the two questions were not, of course, mutually exclusive. To me the results suggested that many ministers' judgment of the *propriety* of dealing with issues hinged on their particular concerns. The survey was conducted by a research seminar at the University of the Pacific.

VII

Protestant Faith in Dialogue:
Some Concluding Observations

Religious liberty has many friends in the modern world. It is an idea which has found increasing acceptance, despite the diversity of ways in which it is understood and applied. Those who oppose this idea live in a time when their consciences are likely to be increasingly troubled, for the denial of religious liberty represents policy which is now on the defensive—and not easily defended.

The preceding pages tried to clarify that it matters *how* the idea of religious liberty is understood and applied. They were written out of my understanding of an authentically Protestant Christian perspective. I must now add that it matters how the continuing conversation on religious liberty is to proceed—both among those who accept the principle but disagree as to its basis, and between those who accept and those who do not accept the principle. Protestant Christians must participate in both kinds of discussion vigorously, charitably, and with all the resources of insight they can summon.

1. The Ecumenical Dialogue

The ecumenical movement, in all its numerous emerging dimensions, presents the most immediate challenges and opportunities for dialogue. The Protestant here confronts two problems: (1) the clarification of his own perspective and (2) the enrichment of the total Christian community with that perspective. The second of these is naturally dependent upon the first. But the clarification of the Protestant point of view on religious liberty is a problem we have only just begun to face, although recent years have at least given us greater insight into the diversity of Protestant viewpoints and the need to struggle toward a basis of religious liberty which is reflective of the deepest theological truths we possess.

I have contended here that it is in the twin aspects of the Protestant principle as criticism of idolatry and as positive expectancy of God's activity that we come closest to our authentic basis. This assertion needs additional scrutiny. It also needs careful application to Protestant policy and practice.

Some will be tempted to proceed too quickly to use the Protestant principle as a club against Roman Catholicism. But Protestants certainly cannot begin to criticize idolatry in that church until they have examined more critically the idolatries into which they have themselves so frequently slipped. Protestants probably sin most volubly in this connection, not by identifying their own churches, programs, and doctrines as the sole channels of divine truth and grace (though one also encounters this often enough) , but by so readily supporting the idolatrous claims of secular state and culture. Protestant culture religion, as this kind of idolatry has sometimes been called, is an urgent problem requiring the constant self-purification of ecumenical dialogue. It should be a cause for sorrow and shame that most Protestant Christians in Germany supported Hitler, that few Protestants opposed the saturation bombing of German and Japanese cities by the Western allies, that Protestant churches in America and Western Europe should so readily and uncritically endorse the self-righteous attitudes of their governments and peoples regarding the Cold War, that churches and Christians should indulge in racism and accept the increasingly materialistic values of all modern civilizations without more question. The ecumenical dialogue provides rich opportunities for self-purification because it brings together Christians with different kinds of blind spots in an atmosphere conducive to mutual criticism and clarification. It is a particularly hopeful sign that the World Council of Churches now has such firm roots on both sides of the "Iron Curtain" and among the uncommitted countries of Asia and Africa. There is already evidence that so broadly based a dialogue and fellowship will provide an excellent context for the mutual strengthening, enrichment, and criticism which all Christians need if they are to avoid bondage to local prejudices and idolatries and if they are to serve as the agents of reconciliation and healing which is required by their calling.

The continuing challenge of this dialogue is to keep it honest and to involve the churches at every level so that it does not restrict itself to a limited number of "ecumaniacs" who are detached from the mainstream in the life of the church. The danger is real. While many Protestants and Orthodox Christians doubtless give passing notice to the assemblies of the World Council of Churches, it may be questioned whether as many as five percent are even aware of conferences such as the National Study Conference on Church and State which was held in the United States in 1964. At best, the ecumenical involvement of the average Christian must be considered marginal.

The exciting new dimension of ecumenical dialogue today is that which involves all three of the major divisions of Christianity: Roman Catholicism, Eastern Orthodoxy, and Protestantism. Religious liberty is an important consideration in this dialogue—partly because all three main branches of Christianity are increasingly committed to it and desirous of achieving a common Christian understanding of its theological meaning, and partly also because it is germane to the way in which the churches treat one another in areas of their respective cultural and political dominance.

In dialogue with Roman Catholicism, Protestant faith can discover resources of correction without which it may remain an impoverished expression of Christianity. Rome has been a principal repository of Christian tradition. It has, moreover, the stewardship of a broad catholicity in time, geography, and doctrinal comprehensiveness. The Protestant principle itself requires a Christian stance of openness to God and a resistance to whatever would close new avenues of divine guidance and grace. But this stance must be nurtured by a rich soil of tradition and experience. Traditionally, Protestantism has sought this nurture primarily in Scripture as the basic witness to Jesus Christ, the Word of God. Protestants properly regard this as the surest foundation and one which they cannot leave entirely without at the same time ceasing to be Christian. But this foundation needs an edifice to complete it. The

Catholic principle points toward that enlargement and enrichment of meaning and also toward the unity without which the Protestant principle must be detached and abstract.

Roman Catholicism can help Protestantism in another way. As we have understood it in this volume, the Protestant faith is by no means to be identified with skepticism. But it must be conceded that any principle of criticism risks reversion to skepticism. Dialogue with Roman Catholicism can serve as a valuable check against that danger.

But the Protestant must also raise serious questions in dialogue with his Roman Catholic friends. As seen in the perspective of the Protestant faith, the tendency in Roman Catholic lands to deny religious liberty has been rooted in the absolute claims of the Roman Catholic Church as repository of authority, grace, and truth. This is glaringly apparent in the archaic (we hope!) formula of "thesis-hypothesis." As we have seen, this formula presupposes the Catholic Church to be the sole repository of truth and grace and logically applies that assumption (1) to demand religious liberty when in minority status and (2) to deny it when in the dominant position. But even among the more irenic, liberal spokesmen of recent Catholicism—men whose sincere commitment to religious liberty cannot be questioned—there remain strong reflections of the absolute claim.

In a recent and noteworthy contribution to Protestant-Catholic dialogue, the late Fr. Gustave Weigel illustrates this point. After outlining the "Protestant principle" in terms which comprehend much of what was said earlier in this book, he proceeds to contrast this with his understanding of the "Catholic principle":

It would run something like this: God, who spoke to Israel, historically became man in Jesus of Nazareth who left his living divine humanity to be truly prolonged in an organized visible society called the Church. If man wants God's salvation he must be incorporated into that society and by sharing its life, he shares the life of Christ who is God as well as man. The Christian man does not experience God immediately except in the special case of the mystics. What he does experience is the sacramental symbol which by divine power ontologically changes the sinner inwardly and totally. The truth of God's revelation is the abiding possession of the consciousness of the society called the Catholic Church, and its divinely empowered organs will express it infallibly and adequately.[1]

Protestant and Catholic principles, he holds, "implicitly deny each other at every point." Arguing that the Catholic Church must claim infallibility, he insists that "if Yahweh is the Absolute who founded a Church to unite men to himself, infallibility is what it would necessarily claim." [2] While Fr. Weigel seeks to understand Protestantism (and possibly does so better than most Protestants!) , and while he acknowledges the contribution of Protestantism, there runs throughout his discussion the idea that there is no real middleground between the infallibility and adequacy of the Church (with its traditions, doctrines, means of grace, and authority) on the one hand and skeptical rootlessness on the other.

It is this assumption of Roman Catholicism, which Fr. Weigel has so clearly expounded, that Protestant witness must emphatically deny. It is not necessary to say that you have *all* the truth in order to say that you have *some* of the truth, and that the truth you have is both important and life-giving even though we still "see through a glass darkly." It is not necessary to say that you know *all* about

God or that your church is the *sole* bearer of his grace in order to affirm that you have experienced God authentically and that your church is *a* bearer of his grace. Roman Catholicism risks idolatry by so explicitly identifying the visible church with the divine, and this risk seems especially clear in the explicit dogma of Papal Infallibility— almost any way one might care to interpret that dogma. Father Weigel is frank enough in arguing that there is no possible accommodation between Protestant and Catholic principles. Union between Protestantism and Catholicism, which he considers unlikely, would have to result from conversion one way or the other. By disputing that either-or approach, it is quite possible that the Protestant may, in effect, be seeking to convert his Catholic brother to the Protestant principle—thus confirming what Fr. Weigel said. But, even if this be so, the Protestant acknowledges that there is in Catholicism a rich witness to Christian faith which will only come closer to that faith as it accepts God's transcendence and judgment even of the church and also as it accepts the possibility that God's clearest word may sometimes be communicated through the least likely of his creatures. I find the main directions of ecumenical dialogue promising in this possibility, although the future is hidden from all of us.

There is a further sense in which the Protestant must contribute to ecumenical dialogue. That is in the reminder that God is also more than the Christian dialogue and the common traditions which it presupposes. The Protestant principle will not permit Protestants to exclude the Jew, the Moslem, the Hindu, the agnostic, or anybody else from his line of vision. It will not permit dialogue with another Christian group to blind the Protestant to still others who also could not live and move and have their being apart from God—however poorly they may be aware of things which the Christian understands. Protestant faith requires that the religious witness of every man be taken seriously, and this does not stop at the boundaries of Christian ecumenical dialogue, nor even Jewish-Christian dialogue.

The Vatican Council's "Declaration on the Relation of the Church to Non-Christian Religions" represents a most encouraging development in this direction—one which may have ramifications in the area of religious liberty which are nearly as decisive as the Council's explicit Declaration in that area. In the Declaration on Non-Christian Religions, the Council made clear that there is a great deal of truth and goodness in all the great world religions. "The Catholic Church," said the Council, "rejects nothing which is true and holy in these religions." The "sincere respect" of the Catholic Church for the teachings and customs of other religions is based upon the view that despite differences from the Church's teachings in many particulars, other religions "often reflect a ray of that Truth which enlightens all men." Although this Declaration, like the Declaration on Religious Freedom, makes clear that it leaves intact the church's claim to bear the ultimate revelation in which the adherents of all faiths must find their own "fullness of religious life," it urges a spirit of love, and it seeks to promote a high level of dialogue between Christians and non-Christians. Moreover, it recognizes that there are large areas of life in which Christians and non-Christians can fruitfully collaborate in the achievement of mutual objectives. The Declaration concludes with a ringing repudiation of all forms of discrimination: "the Church rejects (*reprobat*), as foreign to the mind of Christ, any discrimination against men or harassment of them because of their race, color, condition of life, or religion."

Statements such as these, invested as they are with the

full authority of Council and pope, can only be interpreted as strong evidence of a new openness which ought to challenge the imagination of Catholics and Protestants alike. In this spirit of openness, the Protestant must seek a dialogue which also includes persons who fall outside the Christian and Hebrew traditions, and for reasons which have been expressed even more strongly in the present work than in the Declaration.

2. The Dialogue with Marxism

For Protestants, dialogue will continue to be most difficult when it is with those who are in principle opposed to religious liberty. Such people are generally opposed to the idea because they do not consider other viewpoints worth hearing. But dialogue is always two-sided. One cannot, to be sure, enter into dialogue without firm, basic convictions. But dialogue is also unreal unless one expects to encounter other viewpoints which are worth listening to. Happily, a certain hardness has already melted in Protestant-Eastern Orthodox-Roman Catholic relationships, and dialogue there is beginning to move like a torrent. But it remains difficult for Christians to converse with certain other groups who could scarcely care less about conversation with viewpoints differing from their own.

In the contemporary world this problem is best illustrated by Marxism, the one philosophy which continues to lie behind widespread, systematic denial of religious liberty. While the church continues to exist in all the Marxist lands and even to thrive in some, its existence is typically clouded by legal disabilities. The U.S.S.R. is characteristic of the more tolerant Communist arrangements for religion. In Russia there are specific constitutional guarantees of freedom of worship, and some provision has even been made for the upkeep of churches and theological seminaries. But even in the U.S.S.R., freedom of *worship* is constitutionally contrasted with freedom for atheistic *propaganda*, thus emphasizing that non-Marxist religions do not enjoy the same freedom of expression, the same access to media of communication with the public at large. This situation is emphasized by difficulties of the churches in finding publication outlets and in the social disabilities faced by those who publicly avow support of a non-Marxist religion.

In Marxist theory, religion is understood as (1) the hypocritical justification which a governing class supplies to legitimate its exploitation of the exploited class, and (2) the illusory reality (an "opiate") which makes life bearable for the exploited class.

Religious distress is at the same time the *expression* of real distress and the *protest* against real distress. Religion is the sigh of the oppressed creature, the heart of a heartless world, just as it is the spirit of an unspiritual situation. It is the *opium* of the people.[3]

The fact that prior to the development of class consciousness the exploited proletarian class has had need precisely of such opium (a positive note which escapes those who see the figure only as a term of derision) does not change the need to abolish religion "as the *illusory* happiness of the people" for the sake of "their *real* happiness." Accordingly, "criticism of religion is the premise of all criticism," because it points to the most fundamental criticism of the social conditions which occasion the need for such an opium. Religion, therefore, is not only useless to the liberated proletariat; it is fundamentally in error. And it is not only *an* error; it is the *most basic* error.

On the basis of such an unpromising attitude, how can

the Protestant Christian engage in dialogue with Marxism respecting religious liberty?

Practically speaking, many Christians in Marxist lands have long ago begun to develop considerable experience with such dialogue.[4] Common to their experience has been the fact that individual Marxists very often can be reached through the ultimate personal questions of life and death and meaning for which Marxism supplies only shallow answers. Moreover, Christians living in Marxist societies sometimes find that they no longer need to bear the burden of being identified with what the Marxist considers an exploiting class. From a position of weakness they can better communicate without the suspicion that they are simply attempting to justify their class interests. They are also in a better position to raise questions about what Professor Bennett has called "Communist Atheistic Absolutism," the dogmatic Marxist certainty regarding ultimate reality which Bennett properly considers to be idolatrous.[5]

Protestant faith speaks directly to this point. In criticism, it must question the absolutism of Marxist thought with its consequent idolatry. At this point, paradoxically, Protestant faith is much more supportive of the true nature of science than is this "scientific materialism." As Helmut Gollwitzer has said of Marxist materialism, "the transition from methodical to dogmatic materialism means the subjection of science (and so of all intellectual life) to the claims of the arrogant ideological requirements of faith, instead of the former subjection of science to the patronage of the church." [6] This criticism would seem applicable to all attempts to base dogmatic atheism on science, just as it questions all idolatrous efforts by any church to impede full scientific exploration of God's universe.

Many Christian interpreters have suggested, wisely, I think, that the criticism of Marxist absolutism can best be approached through discussion of the nature of man. Marxism can supply only weak answers to the questions, (1) How is it possible for man to have such absolute answers? and (2) What ground is there for assuming that men will be morally perfect in the classless society? A corollary question, which is extremely important in the international political dialogue involving the Communist countries through the United Nations and elsewhere, is this: What is there about man that makes it possible to ignore the issue of *permanent* political structures to serve the responsible society? The lack of theoretical Marxist commitment to the responsible *state* is one of the present frustrations of efforts to organize the world community politically. And this, of course, roots in what must be considered an extremely naïve view of the nature of man. Full exposition of these and other points of criticism obviously cannot be undertaken here, but this may suggest how the Protestant faith can function critically in dialogue with Marxism.

But Protestant faith has other implications in relation to this dialogue. It must criticize tendencies by Christians to use their faith as justification of self-interest wherever such tendencies exist (which may be just about everywhere), remembering that no dialogue with Marxism will be possible where Christian contributions can too readily be interpreted cynically. It must criticize the *absolute* rejection of Marxism by Christians, because Marxism like every other religious or philosophical viewpoint contains much of truth. Indeed, the fundamental attitude of Western Christians toward Marxism has generally been so hostile that there seems little danger of the church's becoming too positive in its appraisal of those truths which are borne by Marxism! While the idolatry of Marxism must be criticized and its shortcuts to power resisted, it is possible that this movement bears an important judgment upon the church and Western civilization which can be ignored only at our peril.

This must lead to the observation that Western Christians can hardly seek to engage Marxism in dialogue internationally or in Marxist lands if they are unwilling to accord freedom of expression to Marxists within their own countries. Their failure to do so in countries such as the United States is fairly patent—even to the point where speakers or writers who only *seem* to be Marxist may suffer serious social and even political disabilities. During the "McCarthy era" of the early 1950's especially, and on a sporadic basis subsequently, persons suspected of Communist involvement have often been hounded ruthlessly. Governmental employees have lost their jobs, teachers have been dismissed, and even clergymen have been interrogated by Congressional committees. Communists themselves have sometimes been imprisoned. Such things have been more fully described by others, but here it must again be said that the Protestant faith requires freedom of expression. It is highly questionable whether Christians in Russia or China are treated any worse than Marxists are treated in the United States, and to the extent of their inhibitions of full freedom of expression both situations are to be considered shameful in the light of Protestant faith.

A question must be raised, however. Does the principle of religious liberty require freedom of expression for those who themselves do not believe in freedom of expression for their opponents? Must a responsible state tolerate the intolerant? Must it provide a platform for those who may use that platform to organize the destruction of such a state? In the case of a Communist who accepts the full Leninist-Marxist view and who is actively related to the Communist Party, the question may not be entirely

241

gratuitous. The suspicion lingers, moreover, that such persons are actively seeking to advance the objectives of foreign Communist powers.

I think one must simply say this: Anybody who is apprehended in an act of crime may properly be prosecuted and tried. But a democratic society must permit even those who are its theoretical opponents the right to speak. In this, I would rather agree with Sidney Hook when he writes that

so far as the logic of the situation is concerned, there is no inconsistency in tolerating the expression of all religious opinions including the *opinion,* as distinct from current practice, that the true religious faith justifies in the future repression of religious error. Such an opinion is undoubtedly a powerful reason for not subscribing to such a religion; by itself it is not sufficient ground for legal interdictment of the profession of the religion. If a group promises some day to interfere with our religious freedom but scrupulously refrains from doing so now, our duty is to agitate and educate to prevent them from winning political power to carry out their threat to our religious freedom. It is not to violate their religious freedom now.[7]

This is to say that freedom of expression should include freedom to judge democracy and the faiths which sustain democracy themselves. Moreover, it suggests that a responsible state must be open to the idea that a better kind of state is in principle possible. Thus it must accept the *possibility* that its last (and fulfilling) act would be to facilitate a peaceful transition to such a superior system. It is properly skeptical, of course, that such a superior system could exist. And accordingly it properly renders the mechanics of such transition more difficult than the bare majority rule typically required of most of its lesser decisions.

But this kind of openness serves one very important practical function. It forces those who are enemies of freedom to give rational account of themselves in the broad light of day. More positively, it makes it possible for such persons to be brought into a position where they may themselves see that violence and repression are irresponsible means of social change.

3. The Dialogue with Secular Humanism

The concern of this work has been to affirm religious liberty and to search out the deepest Christian things that can be said in support of it. By implication, the attack has been centered upon those who deny religious liberty either theoretically or practically and those whose theological justification for it is considered to be inadequate.

It should not be overlooked, however, that secular humanists, who often pride themselves on *alone* being principled in their support of freedom may not unambiguously be so. Secular humanism, whether it derives from forms of scientism, logical positivism, existentialism, cultural relativism, or linguistic analysis, is likely to represent a specifically "post-Christian" viewpoint. In Western countries, at least, its representatives have often had early exposure to Christian or Jewish religion, which they have subsequently rejected in favor of one of the secular value systems. While such people generally consider themselves to be democratic and freedom-loving, they may also consider Christianity or Judaism to be unworthy of further consideration in a more enlightened age. The attitude is suggested by the following quotation from an article in the *Humanist World Digest:*

Here lies one of the essential differences between our religion and that of others. Instead of basing our attitude toward life upon a dogma, a spiritual assumption, or an imaginary law of God, we based it upon life itself. Instead of answering problems with a text from the Bible, we solve them in the light of verified knowledge of the physical, intellectual, and moral constitution of man.[8]

"In the past," the writer goes on rather sweepingly, "the fears and the hopes alike of religion taught man to deny life, to despise it, to evade it. . . . But our religion is one which says 'yea' to life here and now." While in the same article he asserts that humanistic religion "must always be a religion with an open mind," it is quite apparent that his mind is closed to the possibility of any value in most of the religious heritage of mankind. These few quotations would suggest the basis for some engaging dialogue between such a humanistic viewpoint and the theological perspective of a Niebuhr or a Tillich.

In the absence of such dialogue, secular humanism may, in subtle but real ways, contribute to policies which undercut the full opportunity of other religious faiths (which have been dismissed as superstition or spiritual tyranny) to express themselves. This could be true, for instance, wherever public education is in fact determined to maintain a secularistic point of view. The Protestant faith must always remind secular humanism that its "absolutes" are no less shaky than those of the Christian tradition and that they may indeed be more so.

Gandhi, whose credentials as a lover of freedom and democracy can hardly be contested, supplies an intriguing illustration of how an implicit opposition to religion can affect public policy. Referring to Western missionary efforts in India, he once wrote that current missionary activities are of three kinds, good works, education and religious propaganda. In the India of tomorrow the first two will be allowed to go on without hindrance and will even be welcome but, if the missionaries continue to bend their efforts towards religious proselytizing through medical and educational work and so on, I shall certainly insist that they leave free India. The religions of India are right for her people: we have no need of spiritual conversion.[9]

The irony of the term "free India" in combination with the dogmatism of the concluding sentence must have escaped that great man! But those who hold the Protestant faith must insist upon freedom for all kinds of proselytizing efforts everywhere—even those designed to turn Protestants into something else. In the deepest sense, the free expression of religious witness is necessary in every society. And certainly "freedom" is an empty term if it does not also apply to proselytizing efforts on behalf of viewpoints we do not find attractive.

The points raised in this study may help open dialogue with those who do not share the Christian faith but who do have a genuine commitment to freedom. Here they may discover that Christians can in principle be loyal friends of freedom. As they consider the ultimate ground upon which Christians base their commitment to freedom, they may be challenged to give their own commitments deeply positive as well as negative significance. Is their love of freedom based only upon a rejection of a religious faith which is currently in a position of power, or do they find something affirmative in humanity or the nature of being itself which requires the freedom of all for it to be fulfilled? This is the question which the Christian must pose to the secularist.

One may venture the hope that in dialogue with secular humanism Christians who are committed to religious liberty in the full sense described in this book may find wider opportunities of witness to their faith itself than they could have predicted.

4. Dialogue as Means and Dialogue as End

Through dialogue the Protestant faith attempts to gain more and better friends for religious liberty. Wherever Protestant Christians enter into dialogue with others, they must do so partly to advance this objective and in the hope that it may be made secure in law and tradition in the present generation. The objective is not simply a Christian concern; it is a universal human one. But it is a concern which the Christian thinks he understands particularly well from the vantage point of his faith—especially as this is interpreted in the light of the Protestant principle. Quite possibly, what really happens in the modern world with respect to religious liberty will depend upon how well the Protestant enters into this dialogue. In the spirit of the Protestant faith every participant in the dialogue finds himself and his religious commitments taken seriously and as one who in some sense is also a bearer of ultimate truth.

Finally it needs to be said that Christians do not enter into dialogue simply as a means to some other end. Dialogue itself, in both its intellectual and spiritual forms and in its divine-human and man-to-man dimensions, is an end in itself. Where people enter into dialogue authentically, the Protestant principle is already expressing itself in an important sense—for real dialogue takes both truth and error and both good and evil most seriously. Where people are drawn into authentic dialogue, a conversation committed to truth and goodness, the sovereign God is best able to make himself known.

Religious liberty is the social policy which seeks to

facilitate God's access to all through the free witness of all. It is a highway for God which man must build and maintain.

NOTES

[1] Robert McAfee Brown and Gustave Weigel, S. J., *An American Dialogue* (Garden City, N.Y.: Doubleday, 1960), pp. 191-92.

[2] *Ibid.*, p. 181.

[3] This and the following quotations are from the essay by Marx, *Toward the Critique of Hegel's Philosophy of Right,* which was first published in 1844 in the *Deutsch-Französische Jahrbücher.*

[4] Writings by Charles C. West, Helmut Gollwitzer, and Johannes Hamel have portrayed this with considerable vividness.

[5] John C. Bennett, *Christianity and Communism Today,* pp. 81-85.

[6] Helmut Gollwitzer, *The Demands of Freedom* (New York: Harper & Row, 1965), p. 146.

[7] Sidney Hook, *The Paradoxes of Freedom,* p. 135.

[8] John H. Dietrich, "Who Are These Agnostic Humanists," in *Humanist World Digest,* XXVI, No. 1 (1954), 7.

[9] Quoted in A. F. Carrillo de Albornoz, *Roman Catholicism and Religious Liberty,* p. 25.

INDEX